BIG BOOK OF THINGS TO KNOW

Sarah Hull, Laura Cowan
and James Maclaine

Illustrated by Susanna Rumiz, Alyssa Gonzalez,
Carolina Búzio and Paul Boston

Designed by Katie Webb, Emily Barden,
Jenny Hastings and Lenka Jones

USBORNE QUICKLINKS

Scan the code for links to websites
with exciting videos, activities and facts,
or go to **usborne.com/Quicklinks**
and type in the title of this book.

At Usborne Quicklinks, you can download a map of the world
if you want to find any of the animal places mentioned on
pages 128-189 — and you can also listen to someone
saying the names of all the dinosaurs in this book.

Children should be supervised online.
Please follow the internet safety guidelines at Usborne Quicklinks.

CONTENTS

LOTS OF THINGS
TO KNOW ABOUT...

This book will explain things as you go along. But you'll find lots of useful words explained in the glossary, too.

And there's an index to help you find the things you want to read about.

LOTS OF THINGS
TO KNOW ABOUT
YOUR BODY

All wrapped up

Your brilliant body has thousands of different parts —
some big, some small, some hard, some squishy.
All of these are wrapped up in amazing stuff called **skin**.

Your skin helps hold
your body together...

...but it's stretchy,
so you can move.

And skin is waterproof,
so you don't dry up in
the sunshine, or soak
up water like a sponge
when you swim.

Take a deep breath

Can you feel your chest move out?
Air is rushing into your lungs...

The air blows up
600,000,000 tiny
balloons called alveoli.

ALVEOLI

This is how your
body gets oxygen
from the air.
You need oxygen
to stay alive.

Usually, you do this
about 16 times every
minute – without
thinking about it.

You can probably hold
your breath for about
30 seconds to a minute.

But some trained divers can
hold their breath for as long
as **20 minutes**.

7

Why do you have a belly button?

Your belly button just sits on your tummy, but once upon a time, it **kept you alive**.

Before you were born, you grew for about 9 months inside a warm and cosy womb.

Back then, your belly button was a tube called the umbilical cord.

It brought you food, water and oxygen — everything you needed to grow and stay alive.

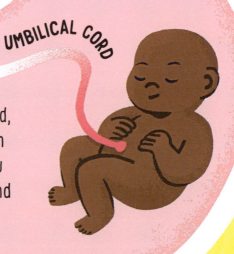

WOMB

UMBILICAL CORD

After you were born, the tube dried up and fell off, but it left a mark behind — your belly button.

Does your belly button stick out, or does it go in?

Babies are WEIRDER than you think...

Babies grow moustaches while they're still in the womb.

The hair is called **lanugo**. When babies have been growing for about four months, it appears on the upper lip, then spreads over the rest of their bodies.

Lanugo usually drops off before the baby is born.

Newborn babies can't cry properly. They make the right noises, but their eyes don't make any tears!

Waaaaaaaaaahh!

It takes about a **month** before a baby's eyes start making tears.

Babies have more bones than you do. Their skeletons have around **300** parts. But as they grow, their bones become harder and some of them join together.

Four bones in the top of the skull join to make one.

BABY'S SKULL

ADULT'S SKULL

By the time you're fully grown, you'll have around **206** bones.

You'll never guess how much you'll eat

Food and drink are the fuel that keeps your body going.
Over your entire life, you'll need **a lot**.

You'll probably eat food weighing more than **five elephants!**

You'll drink enough to fill at least **six concrete mixer trucks**.

Inside your tummy...

...there's a chemical called **hydrochloric acid**. In large amounts, it would be powerful enough to dissolve metal.

This acid is in juices in your stomach. It helps break down tough food, so your body can get the energy out of it.

SALAD

BREAD CRUST

APPLE

FIZZZ...

We're melting!

STOMACH

It also kills germs in food that could make you ill.

POP!

STOMACH JUICES

Why doesn't the acid dissolve my tummy?

MUCUS

Ah. That's because slimy mucus lines your tummy, protecting it from the acid.

11

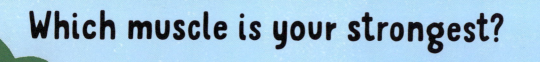

Which muscle is your strongest?

The **hardest-working** muscle in your body is your heart.

It started pumping blood about 8 months before you were born and won't stop until the day you die.

The muscles in the back of your lower legs are **very strong**.

The **biggest** muscles in your body are in your bottom.

They help you stand up after sitting or crouching down.

They pull to keep your body upright and help you stand on tip-toe.

But the **strongest** of all are your jaw muscles, which are incredibly strong for their size.

They help you bite and chew.

Humans have around 650 muscles altogether. These help them move about, talk, eat, breathe...

Only 650? We caterpillars have around 4,000 and we're TINY!

We need all those muscles to pull ourselves along.

Excuse me!

Watch out, it's about to get a little smelly over here...

Farts are a bit rude, but they're completely normal and healthy.

Oops!

Everyone farts around 5–15 times a day...

parp!

...releasing about enough gas to fill a **party balloon**.

How much time you'll spend on the toilet

If you counted up how a typical person spent every single minute of their life, you'd find that they spent...

...over **4 years** eating...

...about **26 years** sleeping...

...around **8 years** watching TV...

...at least **16 weeks** laughing...

...more than **13 years** working...

...around **one year** sitting on the toilet...

...and about **28 years** doing everything else.

All different shapes and sizes

See how the tallest and smallest people ever measure up to an ordinary bed.

Most people fit comfortably in a standard bed...

...but it would have been **far** too short for Robert Pershing Wadlow, one of the tallest people ever to have lived.

I'm the same height as Chandra Bahadur Dangi, the shortest adult ever.

1.6m
(5ft 3in)

54.6cm
(1ft 9½in)

2.72m
(8ft 11in)

Some measurements are the same for **everyone**, whatever size or shape they are.

Spread your arms as wide as they go.

The distance between your fingertips...

...is usually the same as from the top of your head to the soles of your feet.

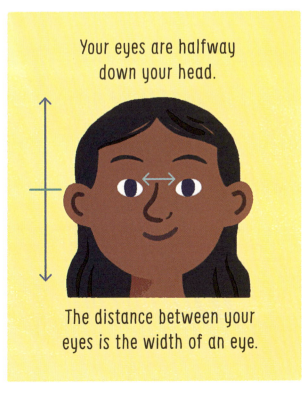

Your eyes are halfway down your head.

The distance between your eyes is the width of an eye.

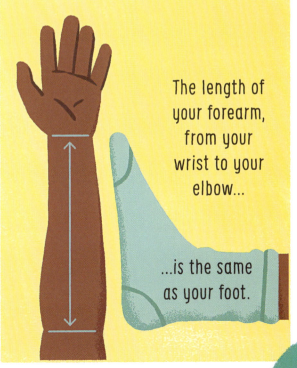

The length of your forearm, from your wrist to your elbow...

...is the same as your foot.

One-of-a-kind prints

Look closely at the ends of your fingers and you'll see patterns of loops, whorls or arches.

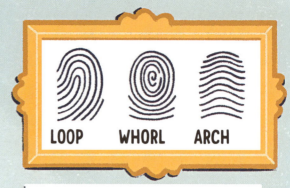

LOOP   WHORL   ARCH

Unknown artist's fingerprints

No one in the whole world has the same fingerprint patterns as you.

Max's right-hand prints

Milo's right-hand prints

MAX

Not even identical twins have the same fingerprints.

Guess what! If you could take a print from your tongue, it would be different from everyone else's too.

MILO

CRIME SCENE

Whenever you touch something, you leave behind faint fingerprints. Fingerprints can help detectives solve a crime.

The only thing the robber took was a eucalyptus plant.

Detectives just have to find someone whose fingerprints match the ones at the scene of a crime.

But maybe detectives shouldn't be looking for a human at all...

It turns out that koala and chimpanzee fingerprints look almost exactly the same as human ones.

It wasn't ME!

You're electric!

There's electricity whizzing around your body all the time. It's used to carry messages to and from the brain.

When you touch something, an electrical message is sent from your fingertips to your brain.

Fluffy!

PING!

CUDDLE IT!

Messages zoom along **really fast** — they're the fastest thing in your body.

PING!

PING!

CUDDLE IT!

Your tongue only knows five tastes

Broccoli, raspberries, chocolate cake and cheese...
These foods are **very** different, but to your tongue,
they're all a mix of just five tastes.

Hello, we're tiny sensors on your tongue called TASTE BUDS. You have thousands of us.

SWEET

SOUR

BITTER

SALTY

Each taste bud tests for one of the five tastes.

UMAMI

The fifth taste is called UMAMI. It's a savoury flavour.

But your taste buds aren't the only things at work when you eat...

That LOOKS good and it SMELLS so chocolatey!

Mmm... so gooey!

Squiiish

Your nose, eyes and mouth work **together** to build up a much fuller picture of what foods are like.

Why Brussels sprouts are yucky

Children are **supertasters**. They have a whopping **30,000** taste buds in their mouths.

All these taste buds make children especially sensitive to bitter tastes — like the ones in Brussels sprouts.

A little bitterness can be yummy, but a lot is disgusting.

BITTER

Ugh, Brussels sprouts are yucky!

No, they're delicious!

Grown-ups only have around **10,000** taste buds, so Brussels sprouts don't taste as bitter to them.

23

Your height changes even when you're fully grown

When you wake up in the morning, you're actually taller than when you went to bed.

During the day, you're on your feet a lot, carrying the weight of your body — and sometimes even more.

That weight squashes the knobbly bones in your back and the bones in your knees closer together.

About this much taller for grown-ups.

At night, when you lie down, they stretch out again.

Space travel makes you taller

In space, your body is almost weightless, so the bones in your back and legs don't get squashed together **at all**. In fact, these bones get further apart.

Astronauts can grow this much taller in space!

After a few months back down on Earth, our heights return to normal.

Why your blood is red

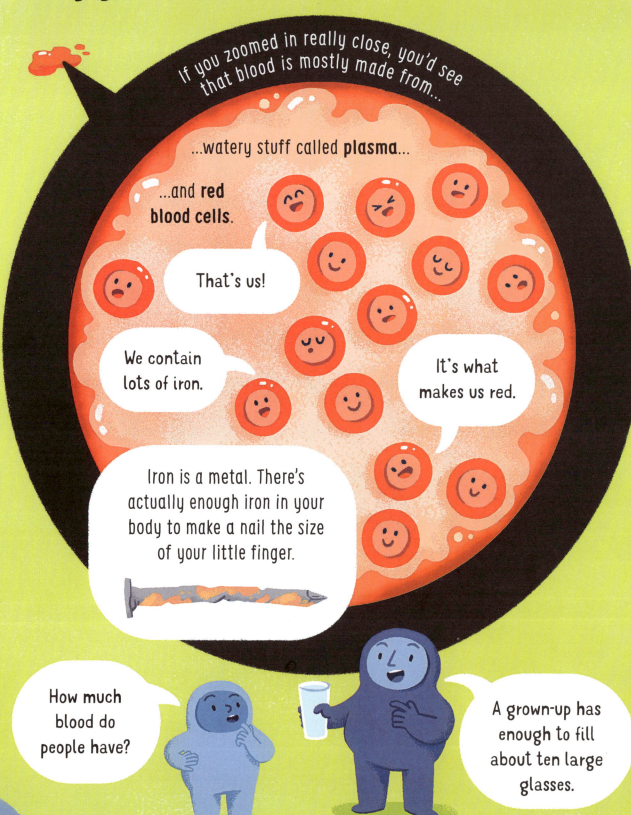

Ba-bump, ba-bump, ba-bump...

Your heart is a muscle. It's about the size of your fist, but it pumps blood **all around** your body, keeping you alive.

Blood flows to every part of your body through tiny tubes.

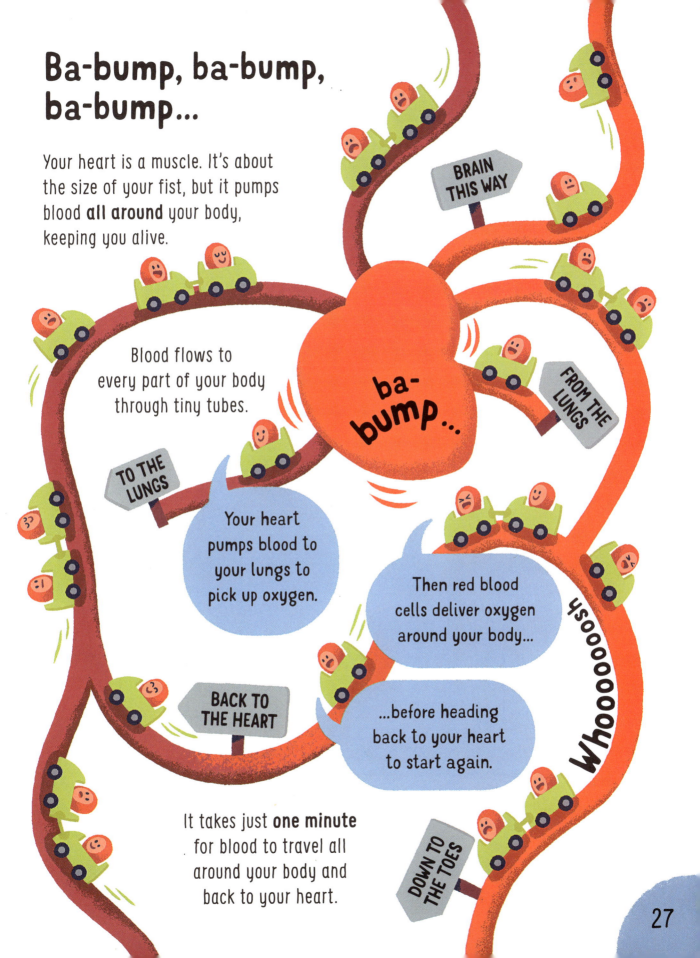

BRAIN THIS WAY

FROM THE LUNGS

TO THE LUNGS

ba-bump...

Your heart pumps blood to your lungs to pick up oxygen.

Then red blood cells deliver oxygen around your body...

...before heading back to your heart to start again.

BACK TO THE HEART

Whooooooosh

DOWN TO THE TOES

It takes just **one minute** for blood to travel all around your body and back to your heart.

Every body needs help with something

The way people's bodies look and work can be very different. Some differences are more obvious than others, but everyone has different strengths and different things they need help with.

I'm blind. That means I can't see. My guide dog helps me get around.

Lots of people need to wear glasses or contact lenses to see clearly — about three people in every four.

Beep beep!

I find it difficult to speak, so I'm using sign language to talk to my friend instead.

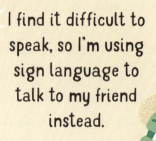

I wear a hearing aid to help me to hear.

Someone who's shy might find it hard to talk to people.

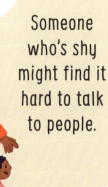

Hi!

I was born with part of my leg missing. I use a prosthetic leg to help me walk and run.

5... 6... 7... 7.50... nearly there... 7.70.

Some people use a crutch, stick, wheelchair or mobility scooter to get around.

The way people's brains work can be different, too. Some might need more time or extra help to learn or do things.

You'll never guess how many facts I know about my body!

Some people might find it hard to sit still and concentrate, but could be full of ideas and brilliant at remembering facts.

You can't always see a disability, so it's important to be kind and patient with everyone.

Vital organs?

Your body has lots of different parts called organs that work together to keep you alive. But you **don't** actually need them all...

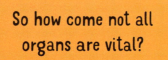

So how come not all organs are vital?

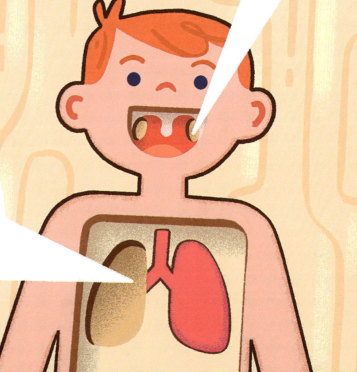

At the back of your mouth, are two bumps — your **tonsils**. They're part of how your body fights off germs, but you don't need them.

People's tonsils are sometimes removed, if they keep getting infected.

Two **lungs** inside your chest breathe for you. But you can survive with one.

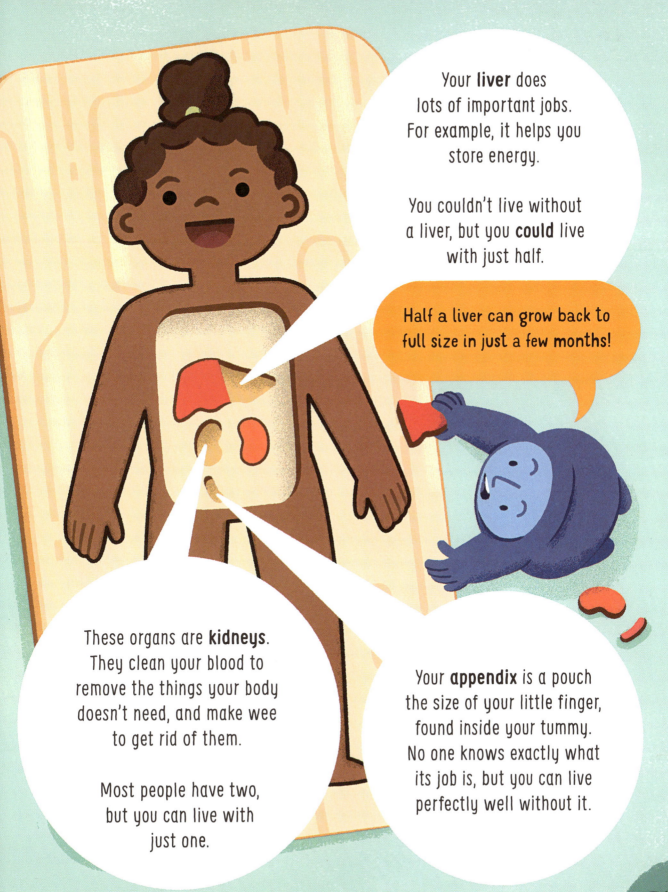

Your **liver** does lots of important jobs. For example, it helps you store energy.

You couldn't live without a liver, but you **could** live with just half.

Half a liver can grow back to full size in just a few **months**!

These organs are **kidneys**. They clean your blood to remove the things your body doesn't need, and make wee to get rid of them.

Most people have two, but you can live with just one.

Your **appendix** is a pouch the size of your little finger, found inside your tummy. No one knows exactly what its job is, but you can live perfectly well without it.

When dust or dirt tickles inside your nose or throat, you might need to sneeze.

A sneeze is an **explosion** of air that sends tiny drops of water and snot flying out of your nose and mouth.

Ahh-choooooooo!

Sneezes burst out at an incredible speed and can travel as far as the length of a bus.

Inside sneeze droplets are extremely small things called germs – like me.

There are THOUSANDS of germs in every sneeze.

We can make you ill.

Yuck! Next time, try to trap it in a tissue.

A LOT of snot

If thinking about snot makes you turn a little... green, **turn the page now!**

Your nose makes a **lot** of snot. But only a **small** amount of it comes out of your nostrils.

I'm stuck!

All this snot is there to trap germs and dirt you breathe in, so they can't cause any problems.

Most snot runs down the back of your nose and into your tummy!

Eugh!

You swallow about one stomach-full of snot every day. The germs get killed in your stomach.

TO THE STOMACH ↓

33

Drink up!

More than half of your body is actually **water**.

Drinking at least six glasses of water every day keeps your body's water supplies topped up.

Your body loses water every day, when you sweat, when you breathe out, and when you go to the toilet.

In hot weather, you can sweat as much as two large glasses of water every hour!

If your body was a bottle, it'd be filled to about here with water.
↓

If you lose more water than you drink, your brain finds it harder to think clearly and your body starts feeling tired. You might even faint.

Water's best, but you can get a lot of water by drinking juice and milk too.

People can only survive for a few days without drinking.

You couldn't live without...

Your body needs all sorts of chemicals to survive. Luckily, your body can get them in just the right amounts from ordinary foods.

Stay healthy with ZINC

Your body needs **zinc** to help fight off germs that cause diseases.

Beans

Eat IRON

Without **iron**, your body couldn't make blood.

Beans

Lentils

Dried apricots

Potassium helps your muscles, including your heart. Without it, things would soon go wrong.

Rich in MAGNESIUM

Your body needs **magnesium** and **calcium** to build strong bones and teeth.

Seeds

POTASSIUM-rich foods here

High in CALCIUM

Bodies worth MILLIONS!

Some people have special talents that rely on a particular part of their body. A few insure these parts for **vast** sums of money.

What does insuring part of your body mean?

Well... if that part was injured, the owner would receive lots of money. Here are some of the amazing body parts that famous people have insured.

FEET

Dancer Michael Flatley's astounding feet set a world record for tap dancing, tapping 35 times in just one second!

TIPPITY

TAPPITY

TAP

$ $ $ $

$ $ $ $

VOICE

Singer Mariah Carey's incredible voice can sing a far wider range of notes than most singers.

I don't want a lot for Christmas...

LEGS

THWUMP!

€€€

Footballer Cristiano Ronaldo's legs have scored well over 750 goals, helping his team to victory.

TASTE BUDS

£ £ £

Hayleigh Curtis is a **chocolate scientist.** Her extra-ordinary taste buds help her invent delicious new types of chocolate.

Mmm... it's got that melt-in-the-mouth texture, but it's a little too sweet.

HANDS

Star pianist Lang Lang's hands dance across the piano keys, making magnificent music.

PLINKITY   TINKLY   PLINK

$$$

You'll never guess who's hairier

A chimpanzee **looks** a lot hairier than a human...

....but humans actually have just as much hair as chimpanzees. It's just that most human hairs are much finer and shorter.

I'm bald, so I can't be as hairy as a chimpanzee.

You are – even bald heads have hair. It's just so short and fine you can barely see it.

The only places your skin is **truly** bald are your lips and the palms of your hands and the soles of your feet.

When it comes to the number of hairs on their heads, some people have more than others.

Redheads have the **fewest** hairs – around 90,000.

People with black hair have about 100,000.

If you have brown hair, you probably have around 110,000.

People with blond hair have the **most** – about 120,000.

Hair is made of strong, stretchy stuff called **keratin**.

All these things are made of keratin too.

CLAWS

HORNS

FINGERNAILS

HOOVES

Around and around the world...

During your life, you'll walk, run or roll a really long way — far enough to take you **three times** around the world.

That's around 170 million steps!

Every step you take uses around 200 muscles.

You'll go EVEN FURTHER if you do lots of sport!

Which is more tiring, standing or walking?

Whether you're walking, dancing or standing still, strong stretchy muscles under your skin are **always working**.

Walking uses **all** the muscles in your legs and feet, but not at the same time. That means they share the work.

I could march like this for hours.

I've only been standing for 10 minutes and my legs are already tired.

When you stand still, some muscles in your feet, legs and back have to work to keep you in position. They don't get any breaks, so can quickly start to ache.

So standing might not look as energetic as walking, but it's actually more tiring.

41

You're a lot like everyone else...

Every single part of you is built following a set of **instructions** called **DNA**.
There's DNA everywhere inside your body.

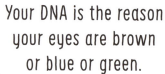

DNA

Your DNA tells your body how tall it should grow.

Your DNA decides whether your hair is curly or straight.

Your DNA is the reason your eyes are brown or blue or green.

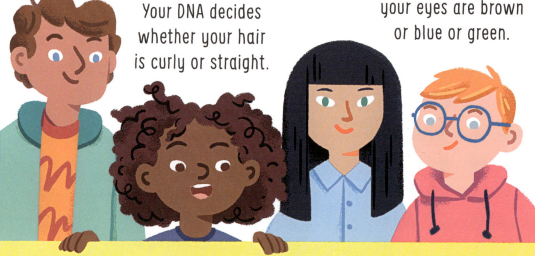

Humans all look **really** different, but when it comes to their DNA, they're almost exactly the same.

This blue part shows how much DNA you share with everyone.

Just this tiny red part is different. It's what makes you **you**.

...and you're *quite* like a banana

It's not just humans that are built according to DNA instructions. **Every** living thing is — from mice and jellyfish, to bananas.

Guess what! Lots of these DNA instructions are the same, whether you're a human, a mouse or a banana.

Only this much DNA makes us different!

You share this much DNA with a mouse.

You share this much DNA with a jellyfish.

And you share this much DNA with a banana!

Remember, remember...

Your brain is about the size of two clenched fists, but it can hold an enormous amount of information.

It has enough memory power to store as much as...

...four billion books...

That's far more books than have ever been published!

...or 300 years of television...

300 MILLION HOURS OF RECORDING REMAINING

...or the entire internet.

Pasta bake

Wow!

You'll never run out of space for new memories!

So why can't I remember EVERYTHING I've ever read or done?

Your brain only stores memories it thinks are important.

How your ears help you balance

Ears help you hear, but they also have another important job...

Deep inside each ear there's a strange tube with three loops that helps you **balance**.

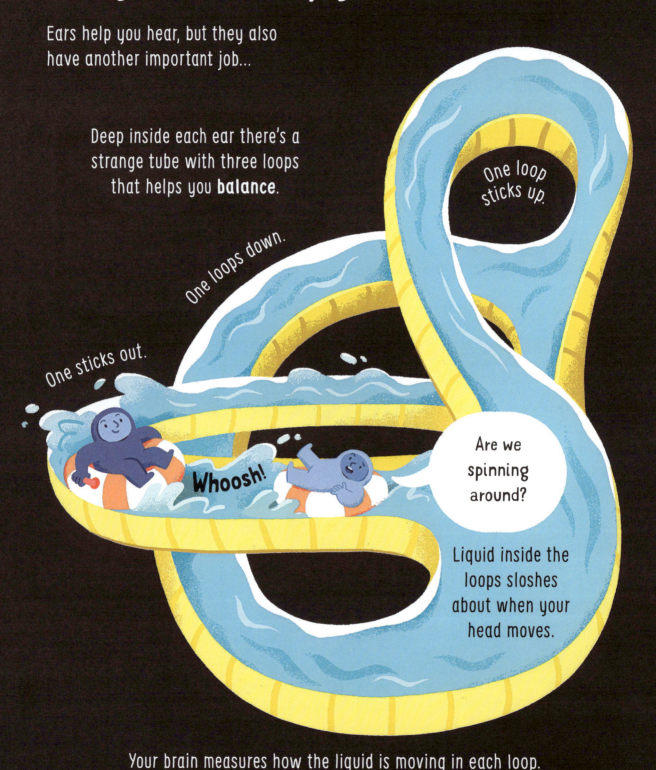

One loop sticks up.

One loops down.

One sticks out.

Whoosh!

Are we spinning around?

Liquid inside the loops sloshes about when your head moves.

Your brain measures how the liquid is moving in each loop. This allows it to keep track of what's up and down, and left and right, and helps you to keep your balance.

46

Have you ever spun around and around?

Wheeee!

I'm so DIZZY!

The liquid in your ears keeps moving for a while after you've stopped spinning. This confuses your sense of what's up and down, right and left.

If the loops in your ears didn't work properly, you would feel like this **all** the time.

You'd probably fall over a lot.

You'd feel dizzy all the time.

And you definitely wouldn't be able to balance on one leg.

Long ago hairdressers cut more than hair

Barbers used to do **surgery** as well as haircuts and shaves.

Europe, 700 years ago...

What can I do for you? Do you need an arm chopped off? Or perhaps you'd like a tooth out?

Argh, no! Just a shave, please.

Back then, surgery was very risky. Many patients didn't survive.

There was no way of numbing pain, so surgery hurt a lot, too.

How long a beard can grow

Beard hairs grow faster than all other human hairs.

In ancient Egypt, beards were a way of showing how important you were. Kings often wore fake beards made of metal. Sometimes queens did too!

If a man never trimmed his beard...

...it would grow as long as **five times** his height in his lifetime.

What's eating your lunch

Inside your tummy there are trillions of tiny living things called bacteria. It might sound icky, but you **need** them!

We bacteria help you DIGEST your food.

That means we break it down to get out the things that give you energy and help you grow.

We get good stuff called vitamins out of fruit and vegetables for you.

I'm good at digesting meat.

Unfortunately, some of these bacteria also make smelly gas.

TOILETS

Everything your body **doesn't** need from food comes out as poo.

Rumbling tummies

Did you know doctors call tummy rumbles **borborygmi** (bore-bore-IG-me)?

These rumbles are the sound of food, stomach juices and gas as they move through the tubes in your tummy.

Gurrrgle rrrumble

Hmm... sounds hungry to me!

A full tummy muffles the noises. If you're hungry and your tummy's empty, rumbles can be **much** louder.

Can you guess what these medical names describe?

SYNCHRONOUS DIAPHRAGMATIC FLUTTER

HIC...
HIC...
HIC...

Hiccups

HORRIPILATION

Goosebumps

SPHENOPALATINE GANGLIONEURALGIA

Brain freeze

Your bones are alive

The bones in museums are old and dry. They're very different from the ones living inside your body.

Those bones look like stones!

Dinosaur bones are SO old that they've become stones called fossils... They're not like YOURS at all.

The outsides of your bones are **really** hard.

Inside, there are lots of **holes**.

This makes your bones strong enough to hold you up, but light enough to carry around.

The holes are filled with a liquid called **bone marrow**. Your blood is made in your bone marrow.

Tiny tubes carry the blood out of your bones and around your body.

Funny bones

X-ray machines can show the bones inside your body. They make black and white pictures like the ones on these pages.

These are the **smallest** bones in your body. They're actually the size shown here.

They're hidden deep inside your ears. They vibrate to **help you hear**.

Did you know you have a **tail**... well, a **tailbone**. It's at the base of your back.

Doctors call this bone the **coccyx** (cok-six).

Coccyx

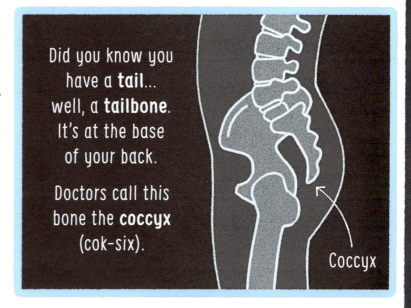

You have the same number of bones in your neck as a giraffe — **seven!**

But the bones in a giraffe's neck are much longer.

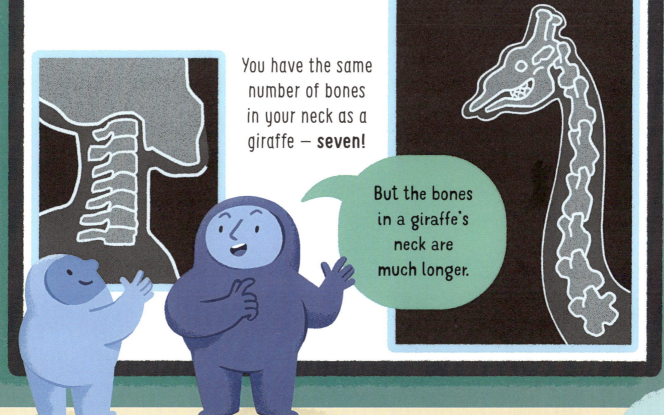

What's that smell?

Scientists think your nose can tell apart at least a **trillion** different smells — that's **1,000,000,000,000!**

Smells help you enjoy food. Most of how food **tastes** is actually down to how it **smells**.

Smells can warn you of **dangers**, such as fire or rotten food that could make you sick.

Your nose can even help you predict the weather.

That earthy smell means a storm is approaching!

Your **body** produces all kinds of smells.

You might notice your body smells different if you eat smelly foods, or haven't washed for a while.

People's smells can change slightly when they are unwell. Humans can't usually detect these smells, but sometimes dogs can...

Dogs' noses can be trained to sniff out diseases.

BLOOD SAMPLES

A
B
C

My human smells a little different before she gets a bad headache.

My nose can sniff out cancer.

I make sure she knows to take medicine, so she won't feel as ill.

What's the time?

Even if you don't know what time it is, your body does. Part of your brain is always keeping time for you. It's known as your **body clock**.

Your body clock controls chemicals called **hormones**. These are sent around your body at different times of the day to tell your body what to do.

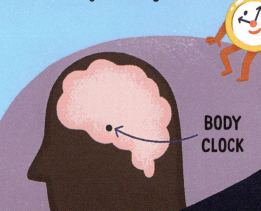

BODY CLOCK

In the morning, your body clock lets your body know it's time to wake up.

DRRRR...

It lets you know it's time to eat...

...and when you have energy to work and play.

When it's time to sleep, your body clock slows down your body, so it can rest.

That's why you can feel so groggy and awful if you're awake when you should be asleep.

But HOW does my body clock know what time it is?

Light. Your eyes detect the cycle of day and night, and set your body clock to match it.

That's why you shouldn't look at screens before bed. Their light can confuse your body clock and make it harder to fall asleep.

OUCH!

Sometimes the place where you feel pain isn't the part that's actually hurt.

When you get brain freeze, the pain in your **head** from eating or drinking something cold actually comes from your **throat**.

People sometimes feel **shoulder** pain when they have a **stomach** problem.

Some people feel the pain of a **heart attack** in their **left arm**.

Problems with **kidneys** can cause pain in the **lower back and thighs**.

Why don't you feel pain in the part that's hurt?

You have pain sensors all over your body. Nerves carry messages about pain from these sensors to your brain. But for some parts of the body, the nerves are connected, so it's easy for your brain to mix them up.

Your brain can't hurt

The only part of your body that doesn't have pain sensors is your **brain**.

Normally, patients are put to sleep before an operation, so they don't feel any pain. But a patient can be kept awake during brain surgery and not feel a thing.

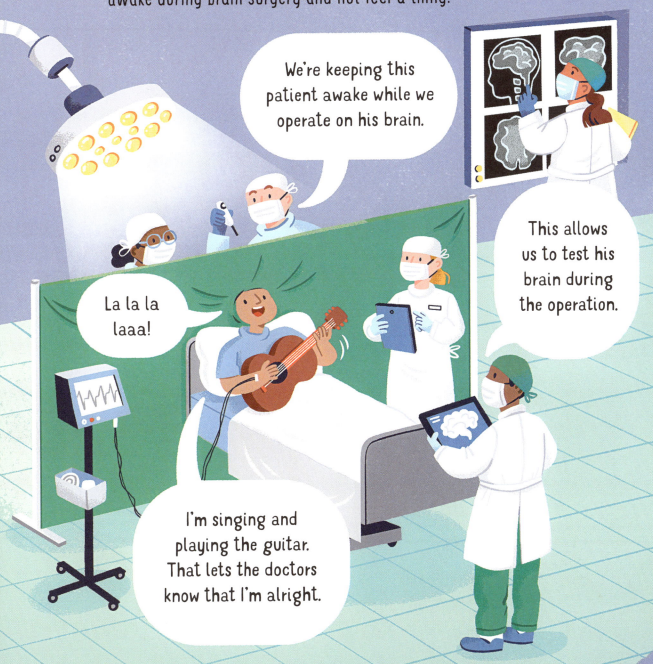

Have a laugh

There are lots of reasons to have a giggle... but did you know that smiling and laughing are actually **good** for you?

When you smile or laugh, your brain releases chemicals called **endorphins**.

Endorphins make you **feel good**. They can even reduce feelings of pain.

Smiling and laughing can bring you **closer to friends** or even help you make new ones.

A proper belly laugh is good **exercise** for muscles in your chest, tummy and shoulders, as well as your heart.

So, after a belly laugh, these muscles feel more **relaxed**.

61

The tiniest things can hurt your body the most

Germs are tiny — **far** too small to see — but if they get inside your body, they can make you ill. Here are some common germs...

SARS-COV-2
Disease: COVID-19

I was discovered in December 2019.

VARICELLA-ZOSTER VIRUS
Disease: CHICKENPOX

We've got NOTHING to do with chicken!

We cause itchy red spots.

INFLUENZA VIRUS
Disease: FLU

STREPTOCOCCUS MUTANS
Disease: TOOTH DECAY

We live on your teeth. Acid we make can damage them.

Loves: sugary foods

Hates: teeth-brushing

CAMPYLOBACTER
Disease: FOOD POISONING

I can give you a sore tummy and diarrhoea.

Loves: raw meat

Hates: being cooked

How your body fights germs

Luckily, your body has its own tiny germ-fighting squad to stop germs from making you ill...

Meet the **white blood cells**.

We travel all around your body, fighting germs.

Some of us attack germs with weapons called antibodies.

ANTIBODY

When the germs are dead, you feel better again.

Some of us gobble germs up...

Burp!

You're about to yawn...

You've probably caught a cold or a cough from someone before, but did you know that you can catch a yawn?

Seeing someone yawn, **reading** the word "yawn" or even just **thinking** about yawning can make you need to...

There are scientific experiments that show you're even **more** likely to catch a yawn if you're told **not** to yawn.

Some people catch yawns more easily than others. Did you make it to the bottom of this page without yawning, or wanting to yawn?

While you're dreaming

You may be asleep when you dream, but your **brain** is hard at work.

It reminds itself about things you've learned during the day.

Your brain is BUSIER at night than during the day.

Pamplemousse

Your brain also files memories away...

Fun at school

Me & Teddy

SCARY

EXIT

And it flushes out waste that collects in your brain while you're awake.

All this helps you stay happy, healthy and ready to learn new things.

LOTS OF THINGS
TO KNOW ABOUT
SPACE

The Moon is really, REALLY far away

Some nights, the Moon looks so close you could touch it.

But it takes about three
days to fly there in
a rocket...

...and it would take over six
months if you could drive
there in a car.

WOWEE!
Tell me
more about
the Moon!

Well, even though it's so
bright and shiny, it doesn't
make its own light. It reflects
the SUN'S light, like a mirror.

The Sun is a star

That's right — a bright, shining **star**, just like the ones you see at night.

It's big and round and hot, just like all stars.

How does it make so much light!?

It's made of hot, HOT gases burning at millions of degrees. It's so enormous, over a million Earths would fit inside!

At over **four billion** years old, the Sun seems old to us, but that's not old for a star. It will keep shining for four billion more.

If aliens sent us a postcard...

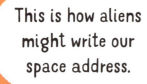

This is how aliens might write our space address.

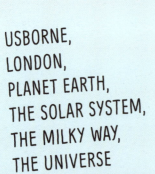

UNIVERSAL POST

Rocketmail

USBORNE,
LONDON,
PLANET EARTH,
THE SOLAR SYSTEM,
THE MILKY WAY,
THE UNIVERSE

We live in space on a massive ball of rock and metal called **Planet Earth**.

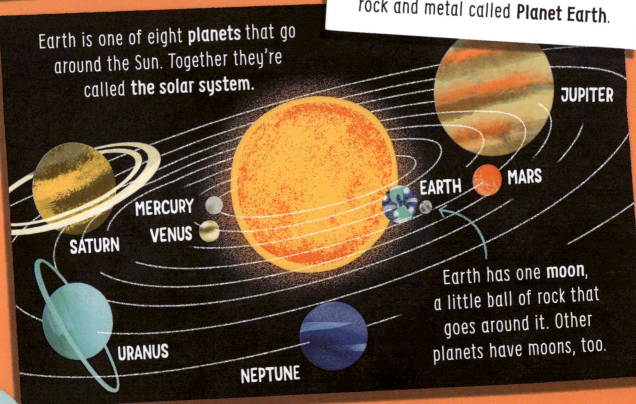

Earth is one of eight **planets** that go around the Sun. Together they're called **the solar system**.

JUPITER

EARTH

MARS

MERCURY

VENUS

SATURN

URANUS

NEPTUNE

Earth has one **moon**, a little ball of rock that goes around it. Other planets have moons, too.

The Sun is one of millions and millions of **stars** spinning together in a group called the **Milky Way**.

Lots of stars have their own planets, too.

This large group of stars is called a **galaxy**. There are lots and lots of other galaxies in outer space.

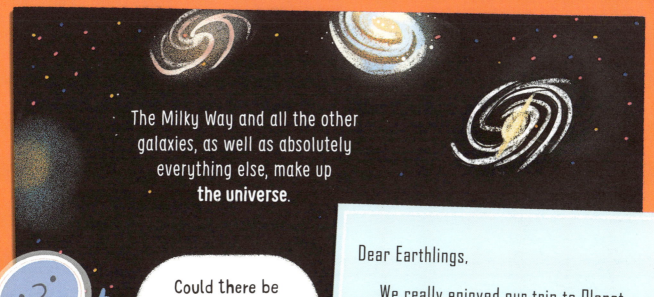

The Milky Way and all the other galaxies, as well as absolutely everything else, make up **the universe**.

Could there be other worlds like ours?

Dear Earthlings,

We really enjoyed our trip to Planet Earth. Thank you for having us and do pay us a visit if you're ever in our galaxy.

Love from your alien friends

Numbering the stars

It's impossible to count every single star in the universe. But **astronomers**, scientists who study the stars, have a pretty good idea how many there are. Here's how they worked it out...

First they counted each point of light in the Milky Way and found **100 billion**.

Next, astronomers worked out how many galaxies are in the universe. They did this by taking very detailed photos of parts of the sky and counting the galaxies they found.

Then they multiplied the number of galaxies by the number of photos they would need to see the whole sky. That made **200 billion** galaxies in the universe!

If each galaxy has around 100 billion stars, that means there are around **200 billion trillion** or **200,000,000,000,000,000,000,000** stars in the universe.

How stars glow

Stars give out different colours of light. The brightest and hottest are blue. Astronomers label each colour of star with a different letter.

O B A F G K M

Our Sun is a **G-type** star.

Earth's next nearest star, Proxima Centauri, is an **M-type** star.

O-type stars are very rare — there are only **20,000** in the whole of the Milky Way!

That's a LOT of stars!

If you look up at the sky on a clear night away from city lights, you might count around **2,500** stars even without a telescope!

Not all astronauts were HUMAN...

Fe, Fi, Fo, Fum and **Phooey** orbited the Moon 75 times in 1972 with American astronaut, **Ronald Evans**.

ORBIT means to go around something.

Fe, Fi, Fo, Fum and Phooey weren't human astronauts — they were **little pocket mice**.

SQUEAK!

These mice were the last living things, including humans, to visit the Moon. But lots of animals have been into space...

Early spacecraft were too small for humans, so scientists sent animals into space instead.

Rats

The first astronauts were **fruit flies**, in 1947.

Guinea pigs

Rabbits

In 1970, the American space agency, **NASA**, sent two **frogs** into space in the **Orbiting Frog Otolith** spacecraft.

Many early astronauts were **dogs**. Scientists trained them to use simple controls in the spacecraft.

Tortoises

32 **monkeys** and **apes** have been to space...

...and an **astrochimp** named **Ham**.

How rain falls on other planets

When rain falls on the Earth, the raindrops are made of water. Other planets don't have much water — or any at all — but it still rains. So, what happens?

On **Neptune**, it rains **diamonds**.

Don't visit **Venus** – it might rain **acid** there.

It rains liquid **methane** on Saturn's moon, **Titan**.

There's even a faraway planet where it could rain **rubies** and **sapphires**.

There's a snowman in space

Far away from Earth, past icy Neptune and Uranus...

...there's a snowman named **Arrokoth**.

It's quite big for a snowman — 33km (21 miles) from head to toe.

Scientists spotted it in the **Kuipur Belt**, a band of icy rocks at the edge of the solar system.

Is Arrokoth REALLY a snowman?

Well, it doesn't have eyes or a carrot for a nose, but it IS made of two icy balls joined together, just like a snowman!

77

Dirty snowballs with long tails

Whizzing around the solar system are dirty snowballs — giant balls of dust, frozen gases and ice that orbit the Sun — known as **comets.**

When a comet passes near the Sun, it starts to melt and loses a lot of its dust and gases.

The dust and gases follow it around in a huge cloud.

When comets get even closer, the Sun's energy pushes the dust and gases into long tails.

The tails can be *super* long — as long as the distance from the Earth to the Sun.

Snowball fireworks

Sometimes the dust left behind by a comet hits the gases that surround the Earth...

Down on the planet, we can sometimes see a kind of firework display in the sky. This is called a **meteor shower.**

Amazing!

A story of looking and learning

There are eight planets in our solar system and lots more objects — but people haven't always known that...

For thousands of years, people studied the skies with only their eyes. They could see Mercury, Venus, Mars, Jupiter and Saturn.

But they only saw them as bright lights in the sky. They couldn't see the difference between planets and stars.

Then in the 1600s, a Dutch spectacles-maker built the first telescope. From then on, astronomers could see those five planets up close.

Does Saturn have EARS?

No, it has RINGS — your telescope just isn't very good!

The new technology helped astronomers to find a few more planets too.

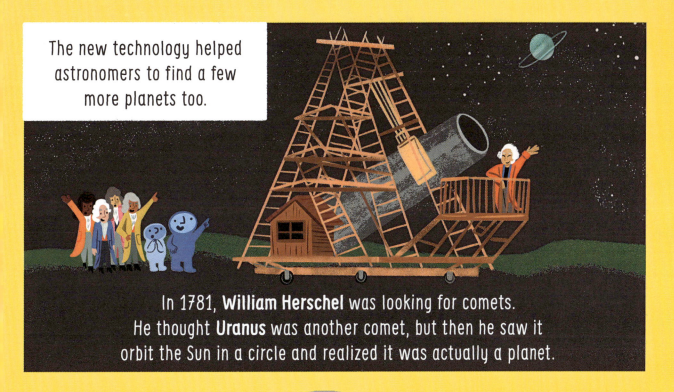

In 1781, **William Herschel** was looking for comets. He thought **Uranus** was another comet, but then he saw it orbit the Sun in a circle and realized it was actually a planet.

There was something odd about Uranus's orbit though — sometimes it was fast and sometimes slow.

In 1842, a mathematician named **Mary Somerville** wondered if another planet — and its gravity — was making Uranus speed up and slow down.

She was right! It was **Neptune**.

Johann Gottfried Galle, **Urbain Le Verrier** and **John Couch Adams** found Neptune in 1846, each working separately. In fact, lots of astronomers had seen it before, but thought it too slow to be a planet.

But Neptune was not the end of the story...

When is a planet not a planet?

In 1930, an astronomer named **Clyde Tombaugh** spotted **Pluto**, orbiting the Sun, just past Neptune. For 70 years, Pluto was thought of as the ninth planet in the solar system.

I'm Pluto. I'm big and round – does that make me a planet?

But, in the 1980s, scientists found out that Pluto was sitting in a band of rocks – the **Kuiper Belt**. There they found more objects very much like Pluto.

Hi!

In 2006, space experts around the world got together to decide – were they **all** planets?

Good day!

Hello!

The first eight planets have all **cleared** their orbits. This means they've pushed out of their way anything in their path – by smashing it into pieces, or picking it up as a moon.

But the little planets in the Kuiper Belt haven't done this. The experts decided that none of them – including Pluto – was a real planet. Instead they called these almost-planets, **dwarf planets**.

Going up!

In the distant future, the cheapest and easiest way to get into space could be a **space elevator**...

It won't be ready for a long time, but scientists in China and Japan are working on ideas right now. What might it be like?

Step into the elevator on Earth and travel to a huge space station. From here, spaceships take you all over the solar system!

Whee!

I'm off to catch a flight to Mars.

Welcome aboard this 07:25 service to Europa.

83

It's oh so quiet up here...

There is no air in space. Without air, sound can't travel, so, however much you shout in space, no one can hear you.

When a star explodes, it does it **silently**.

The **huge** engines on this rocket make a lot of noise on Earth, but **no sound** in space.

If a meteor crashes into a planet with no air, there's **no noise**.

Everyday life in outer space

While you're here on Earth reading this book, there are seven astronauts living on a space station. Life up there is very different...

On Earth, if you jump up, something called **gravity** brings you down again. But that changes when astronauts leave the planet behind.

As soon as they unstrap their seatbelts, they start to float away...

In space, gravity isn't the same as on Earth. Everything feels weightless, so there's no up or down.

Bleurgh, I feel queasy!

Astronauts can't sit down, or walk around the station.

To move, they push and pull themselves along with their hands.

SNORE SNORE SNORE

They sleep in special sleeping bags strapped to the wall.

A lot of their food and drink comes from pouches and tins.

Bread is not allowed — the crumbs could drift off and damage equipment!

There are no space showers. Astronauts use wipes and soaps that don't need rinsing.

Their hair sticks up in all directions!

Astronauts have to go to the gym every day.

Because the gravity is different, their muscles don't have to hold up their bodies in space. So they could become very weak if they didn't exercise.

87

How to use a space toilet

If everything is weightless in space, how do astronauts use the toilet on a space station? It's an important question...

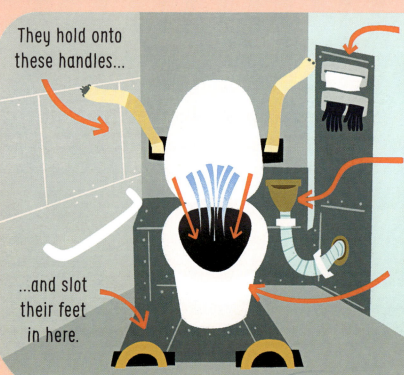

They hold onto these handles...

...and slot their feet in here.

Here are gloves and wipes for cleaning up.

They use this funnel and hose to suck away liquids.

The toilet bowl starts sucking as soon as the lid opens – solids go in here.

What happens next?

Liquids are cleaned and turned into drinking water for the astronauts.

All solids are put in containers that zoom off into space...

PEWWW

...and burn up when they reach the Earth.

From another star system far, far away...

In 2017, an astronomer in Hawaii spotted something amazing. Tumbling past the Sun was a long, narrow, reddish object.

It was too bright to be a comet and moving way too fast to be pulled into the Sun's orbit.

Astronomers realized it was the first thing ever seen that came from outside our solar system.

They named it **'Oumuamua**, (Oh-moo-ah moo-ah) which means **scout** in Hawaiian.

A few scientists think it's possible that 'Oumuamua was made by ALIENS!

REALLY?

Don't take a spaceship to Jupiter

Jupiter is **huge** — twice as big as all the other planets in the solar system put together. It's mostly made of **gases**, so it's known as a **gas giant**.

Landing a spaceship on Jupiter would be impossible, because it doesn't have a solid surface.

In fact, if you did try, your spaceship would sink.

Although the outside of Jupiter is made of gas, the inside is made of **hot**, **hot**, **hot** metal and rock.

If a spaceship sank into the middle of Jupiter, it would be crushed and melted.

The planets that are mushy on the inside

At the edge of the solar system, a long way away from the Sun, are the planets Uranus and Neptune. They're mostly made of heavy gases, known as **ices**, so they're called **ice giants**.

On these extremely chilly planets, hail falls in **mushballs** — ice-covered balls of water and a chemical called **ammonia**.

Pew! Ammonia smells bad. These mushballs STINK!

Where did they all go?

There's no hard ground for the mushballs to land on, so they sink instead. This means the insides of Neptune and Uranus are full of mush!

Baby stars make baby planets...

Baby stars are born from clouds of dust and gas called **star nurseries**.

A baby star spins.

As it spins, the baby star pulls gas, dust and rock into it.

The gas makes the baby star bigger, while the dust and rock spin around it.

Over millions of years, the dust and rock bump and stick together in little clumps.

The little clumps become baby planets. More and more dust and rocks stick to them...

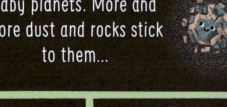

...and they grow bigger...

...and bigger.

Millions — or billions — of years later, they will have grown into big, round planets, all spinning around the star.

...and baby stars eat baby planets

Sometimes a baby star's pull is strong enough to attract a baby planet.

The baby star pulls it closer and closer. Until...

...the baby star **swallows** the baby planet.

Who did it first?

Since the 1960s, humans have been going into space. But who did what first?

The first **spacewalk** was by Russian **Alexei Leonov**, who stayed outside of his spacecraft for 12 minutes.

1968

The first humans ever to **see the far side of the Moon** were the members of the **Apollo 8 crew**. Apollo 8 was one of NASA's Apollo missions to put humans on the Moon.

1965

1961

The first **human** in space was Russian **Yuri Gagarin**.

1963

The first **woman** in space was Russian **Valentina Tereshkova**. Aged 26 at the time, she's still the youngest woman ever to go into space.

2001

The first **space tourist** was billionaire **Dennis Tito**, who paid NASA $20,000,000 to visit the International Space Station (ISS).

2007

US astronaut **Sunita Wiliams** ran the first **marathon** in space.

2015

1969

The first **man on the Moon** was **Neil Armstrong**, closely followed by crewmate **Buzz Aldrin**. No woman has walked on the Moon...yet!

The first **espresso** in space was made using the **ISSpresso** machine and drunk by Italian astronaut **Samantha Cristoforetti**.

What a MESS

Humans have made a big mess on our planet, and they've made one in the space **around** it, too. There's all kinds of **space junk** orbiting the Earth!

Some space junk is big, such as broken satellites and left-behind pieces of rocket.

Some is tiny, such as flecks of paint.

Everything humans leave in space near Earth is pulled into its orbit and that's where it stays. It will never break down.

Altogether there are already tens of thousands of large objects and over a hundred **million** small ones.

Swerve!

The **International Space Station** or **ISS** is a science lab in space. Since the year 2000, astronauts from all over the world have lived and worked there.

Space junk has caused problems for the ISS, because it's all moving **superfast**.

In 2016, a tiny fleck of paint slammed into a window and cracked it.

Imagine the damage a big piece could do!

The ISS has to watch out for space junk, so it can move out of the way.

Everyone should clear up after themselves!

Back on Earth, scientists are thinking up ways to to collect the junk, from harpoons to magnets. But it's a really tricky problem as there's so much of it, and it moves so quickly.

How many people does it take to land on the Moon?

In July, 1969, **NASA**, the American space agency, put the first two humans on the Moon. But thousands more people worked on the Apollo missions that got them there.

Mathematicians calculated the journey to the Moon – and back again!

There weren't many computers in the 1960s. Mathematicians were known as 'human computers' because they worked out everything on paper and in their heads!

Technicians made equipment, such as spacesuits and backpacks, and prepared scientific experiments for the astronauts to do.

Engineers built the spacecraft.

Two astronauts landed
on the Moon...

...while **one** astronaut
stayed in the spacecraft orbiting
the Moon, ready to pick them up.

Back on Earth, there were **20**
mission controllers working in
the main headquarters, Mission
Control, as well as others.

Each mission controller
had a team in **another**
room working for **them**.

Altogether around **400,000** people
worked on the mission.

One million people gathered
at Cape Kennedy, Florida,
USA to watch the Apollo 11
spacecraft lift off...

...and nearly **600 million**
people around the world
watched on their televisions.

Keeping space germ-free

Planet Earth is crawling with teeny, tiny creatures called **germs**. Some of them are good for us and some of them aren't. Either way, it's important they stay on Earth.

Lots of missions are planned to send spacecraft to other planets and moons in our solar system.

One of the things scientists are most excited about is finding signs of life.

They're not expecting to find **big** signs of life, such as alien rabbits, they're looking for **tiny** ones – germs.

In case a planet or moon does have its own germs, it's very important humans don't bring Earth ones.

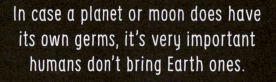

EXTERMINATE!

At worst, the Earth germs could kill off all the alien ones and destroy the chance of more life growing there.

EARTH GERMS — DO NOT LAND HERE!

There are **International Planetary Protection laws** to stop this happening. Mars even has its own **Planetary Protection Officer**.

Sadly, I can only dream of going to Mars – my job is on Earth.

Planetary protection laws protect the Earth, too!

PLEASE LEAVE MARTIAN GERMS ON MARS.

Only the Sun and Mercury are safe from Earth germs. They're so hot nothing could survive there.

The universe awards

Welcome to the universe awards, where the most **extreme** things in the universe are celebrated!

Size

Congratulations to **Mercury**, the **smallest** planet in the solar system...

...and to **Jupiter**, the **biggest**! Outside of the solar system, the biggest and smallest awards are all to play for as more and more planets are discovered.

BIG

HEAT

In the solar system, the surprise winner of the **hottest** planet award is **Venus**!

First I'd like to thank the Sun...

Mercury is nearer the Sun, but Venus has a thick cloud of gas and acid around it, like a blanket that keeps all the heat in.

The **coldest** planet is **Uranus**. Although closer to the Sun than Neptune, it has the coldest ever-recorded temperature of any planet in the solar system – good work, Uranus!

Cold

The **hottest** thing in the universe is a **gamma ray burst**. It's a mega-hot explosion that can happen when stars blow up or collide.

Leaving the solar system far behind, the **coldest** thing in the universe is the **Boomerang Nebula**, a cloud of dust and gas made by a dying star.

The speed of light is the speed limit for the universe. NOTHING can go faster than it can.

The very special prize for the **fastest** thing in the universe goes to... **light.**

SPEED

Drum roll please!

The Sun's light is a wavy rainbow

Sunlight usually looks white, but it's actually made of lots of colours.

The Sun's light travels in waves of different lengths.

The shortest, wiggliest wavelengths look violet.

Indigo

Blue

Green

Yellow

Orange

The longest, widest look red.

The shorter wavelengths are stronger, so carry more of the Sun's heat.

When sunlight shines through rain, the water separates out the waves and you can see a rainbow.

Sunsets on Mars

Welcome to Mars, the **red** planet. There are **red** rocks, **red** dust and, because of all that dust, the sky is **red**, too.

In daytime, the red dust scatters the red, yellow and orange parts of the Sun's light all across the sky.

Just like Earth, the sky changes when the Sun is rising or setting.

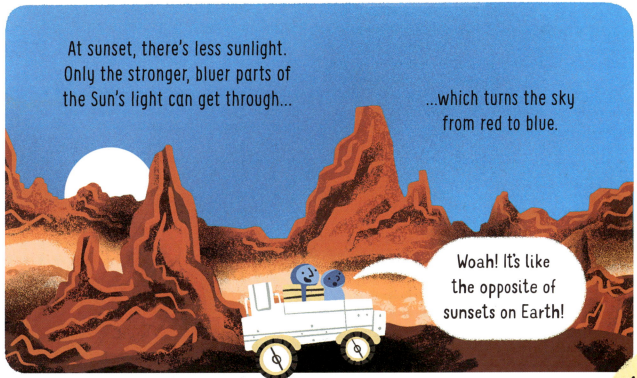

At sunset, there's less sunlight. Only the stronger, bluer parts of the Sun's light can get through...

...which turns the sky from red to blue.

Woah! It's like the opposite of sunsets on Earth!

There's a travel network in our solar system...

It's called the **Interplanetary Transport Network**, but it's not for trains or buses. It's all to do with **gravity**.

The Earth's gravity stops you from floating away. It's what makes things fall down when you drop them.

In space, it's difficult to fly past a planet or a star without being pulled by its gravity. The bigger a star or planet is, the stronger the pull of its gravity.

Spacecraft have to use a lot of power to avoid a planet or star's gravity.

Actually, EVERYTHING has its own gravity – even us! We're just too small for our gravity to be very strong.

Neowww!

So mathematicians have worked out the easiest paths through our solar system — the ones that need the least power.

The paths use points where the gravity of two planets cancel each other out. At other points, a planet's gravity can help a spaceship to speed up or change course.

When scientists launch spacecraft to explore outer space, they send them along these paths — on the Interplanetary Transport Network.

Planet hunters

Astronomers often find new stars using telescopes, but spotting new planets isn't so easy...

Planets don't make their own light — they can only reflect light from a star. But stars are **so** bright, they hide planets in their glare.

That means it's very hard for astronomers to spot faraway planets with a telescope — even a super-strong one.

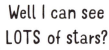

Well I can see LOTS of stars?

VIEW THROUGH A TELESCOPE

But, they can attach something called a **coronagraph** to their telescopes. This removes a star's glare and reveals any hidden planets.

Hiya

VIEW WITH A CORONAGRAPH

Planets outside the solar system are called **exoplanets**, and there are a few clues astronomers can look out for to find new ones.

Shadows
When a planet moves between the star and the person looking at it, the star's light seems to dim a little.

Wobbles
If a star wobbles and flickers, it might be because a nearby planet's gravity is throwing it off balance.

Wonky orbits
Stars travel in orbits, too — sometimes they even orbit each other. If scientists spot a star with an unbalanced orbit, it might be because the star is orbiting with lots of planets, pulling it off course.

Ocean worlds

Earth is the only planet in our solar system with liquid water on its surface. Planets and moons with lots of water are known as **ocean worlds**. Ocean worlds are especially interesting — but why?

Because, on Earth, the oceans are teeming with life.

Earthlings depend on water – even their bodies are full of it!

In fact, the oceans are where all life on Earth began!

Scientists think there could be lots more ocean worlds in our galaxy.

Who knows? Some of them could even be home to other forms of life.

The secret behind a moon's wobble

The planet Saturn has over 80 moons, and even more tiny moons, called **moonlets**.

One of Saturn's moons is called **Enceladus** and it has a secret...

Astronomers noticed that Enceladus wobbles slightly as it orbits Saturn.

Wergh! Uh oh!

They realized the wobble might be caused by a hidden ocean sloshing around deep below the moon's icy surface.

It's not the only secret ocean in our solar system — many of Saturn and Jupiter's moons hide ice-covered seas.

Could there be life HERE?

Robot space adventurers

Humans haven't been to Mars yet, but they have sent intrepid robots, known as **rovers** to explore. This means whenever human adventurers do land there, they will know what to expect.

Each rover explores a different part of the planet. They study everything from weather to rocks, and send information back to Earth.

Life on Mars is hard. The rovers must work through ice, burning sunlight and dust storms.

I can collect lots of soil in my three scoops!

CURIOSITY

Inside one of the rovers is an instrument called a **CheMin**. It works out what's in the soil.

Meet **Spirit** and **Opportunity**, twin rovers, sent to opposite sides of Mars.

We've found rocks that show Mars used to have lakes, rivers and even a salty sea.

This rover is looking for signs that very tiny creatures, such as germs, once lived here.

Sometimes I use my MEGA laser to zap rocks.

PERSEVERANCE

Perseverance drills into the ground and fills tubes with what it finds.

It seals the tubes and leaves them on the surface. When humans finally get to Mars, they can have a look.

How to garden on the Moon

If humans want to travel further into space, they'll need to be able to grow their own food. Plants are used to living on Earth — but can they grow in space, too?

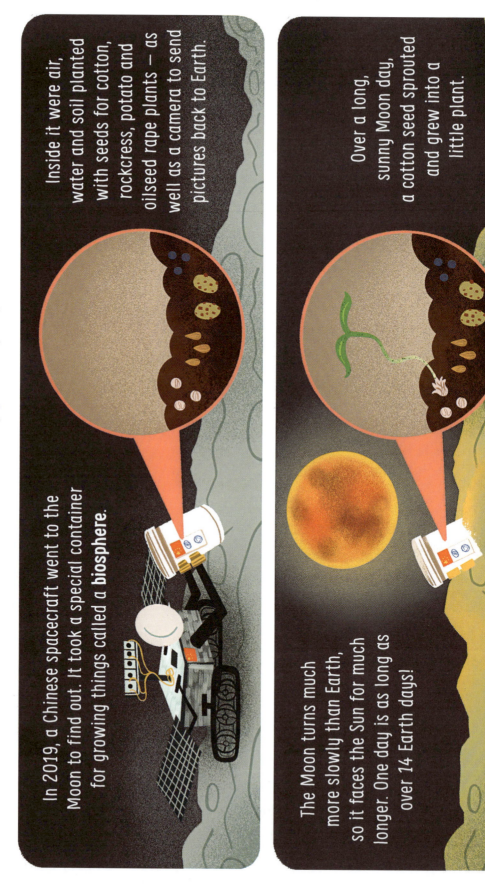

In 2019, a Chinese spacecraft went to the Moon to find out. It took a special container for growing things called a **biosphere**.

Inside it were air, water and soil planted with seeds for cotton, rockcress, potato and oilseed rape plants — as well as a camera to send pictures back to Earth.

The Moon turns much more slowly than Earth, so it faces the Sun for much longer. One day is as long as over 14 Earth days!

Over a long, sunny Moon day, a cotton seed sprouted and grew into a little plant.

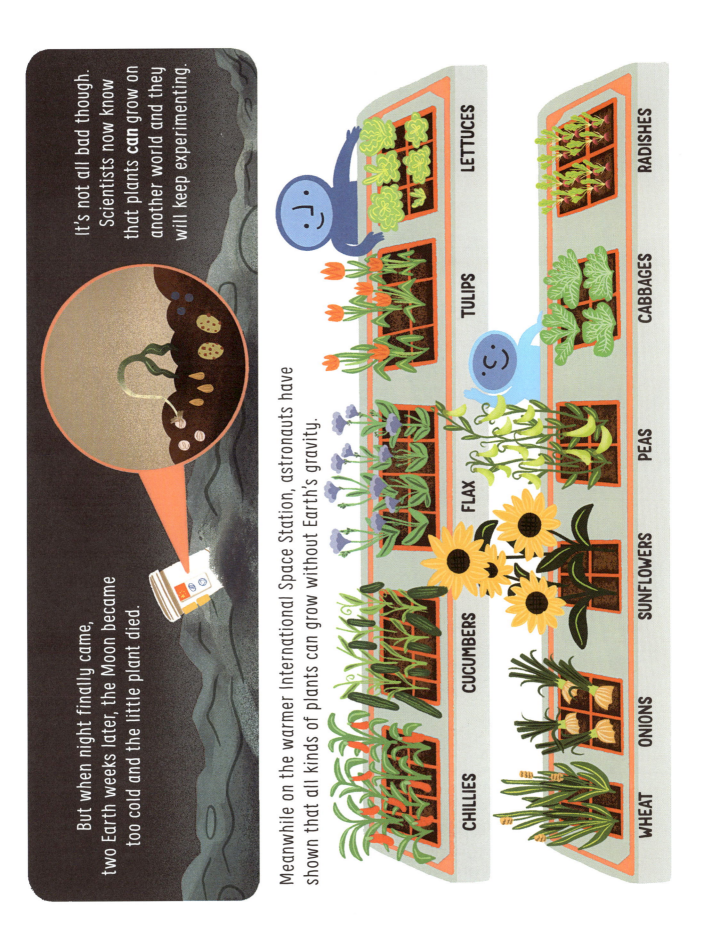

But when night finally came, two Earth weeks later, the Moon became too cold and the little plant died.

It's not all bad though. Scientists now know that plants **can** grow on another world and they will keep experimenting.

Meanwhile on the warmer International Space Station, astronauts have shown that all kinds of plants can grow without Earth's gravity.

LETTUCES

TULIPS

FLAX

CUCUMBERS

CHILLIES

RADISHES

CABBAGES

PEAS

SUNFLOWERS

ONIONS

WHEAT

Measuring the universe

Space is so big, scientists can't use the measurements they use on Earth. So to measure how far away things are outside our solar system, they use the speed of the fastest thing in the universe — **light**.

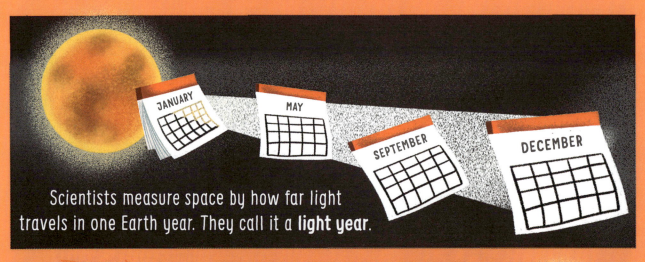

Scientists measure space by how far light travels in one Earth year. They call it a **light year**.

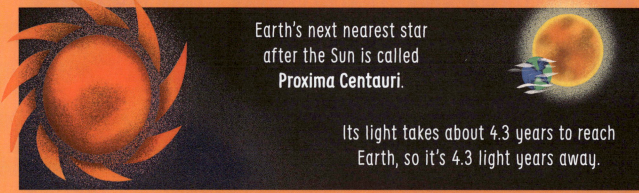

Earth's next nearest star after the Sun is called **Proxima Centauri**.

Its light takes about 4.3 years to reach Earth, so it's 4.3 light years away.

Can we drive to Proxima Centauri?

No, silly, cars don't go into space! And the journey would take over 48 MILLION years!

Even our fastest spacecraft would take about **18,500** years to get there!

Light-distant chatting

If humans ever go to Mars, there might be a hitch when they want to phone home...

Earth and Mars orbit the Sun at different speeds. This means that they are sometimes near...

...and sometimes far away from each other.

Humans can send information — in phone calls or video chats — at the speed of light.

It takes between three and 22 minutes for light (or information) to travel from Mars to Earth...

...so conversations wouldn't be very snappy.

I'm just watching the Martian sunset. It's SO amazing... and... hello?

Yawn... um, so did you tell me what a Martian sunset looks like?

EARTH, 22 MINUTES LATER...

Moon trees

In 1971, astronaut **Stuart Roosa** took a little bag of seeds into space and flew around the Moon with them to see if being in space changed them.

There were 500 seeds from five types of tree.

PINE

So nice of you to visit!

REDWOOD

SWEETGUM

AMERICAN SYCAMORE

FIR

When the seeds came back to Earth, they were planted all over the world, but no one kept a record of **where**. Is there a Moon tree near you? Some of them have a little plaque!

Going to space had no affect on the seeds – Earth trees and Moon trees are exactly the same.

Colds are even worse in space

Catching a cold can make you feel pretty miserable — blocked nose, fuzzy head, itchy eyes. But in space it's even worse.

Without any gravity to drain the snot, it just sits in your nose, making you feel terrible.

And imagine what happens if an astronaut sneezes!?

In 1968, an astronaut went into space with a cold and he gave it to everyone else on the mission!

Now astronauts have to stay away from other people for around two weeks before going into space, to make sure they're not sick. This is called **quarantine**.

Set sail for the stars!

It takes lots of fuel just to go to the Moon. And there's nowhere to refuel, so how can humans ever go any deeper into space?

Well, scientists think **sailing** could be the answer. No one's made a sailing spaceship yet, but here's how one might work in the future.

Sailing ships don't need lots of fuel. The wind blows their sails and off they go!

But where's the wind in space?

Stars are made of
burning gases. Some of the
gases escape and blow away.
This is called **stellar wind**.

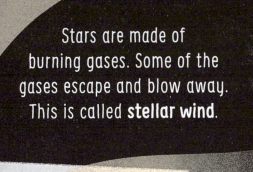

When gases blow away
from the Sun, they're
called **solar wind**.

In the future, spaceships
could be fitted with special
sails so that solar wind could
blow them all the way out
of the solar system.

Our galaxy is bubbly

Some **massive** stars have bubbles round them.
The bubbles are made of stellar wind.

Exploding stars make bubbles, too.

Around the bubbles is a thin,
strong shell made from gas and
dust squashed together. These
bubbles can never burst.

When bubbles squidge together, they make an enormous bubble called a **superbubble**.

Superbubbles are hundreds of light years across and full of gas.

Our solar system has been flying through a superbubble for millions of years. It's called the **Local Bubble.**

There are lots of other stars in the Local Bubble. Baby ones are forming from the gas and dust on its shell.

Telescope time machine

For hundreds of years, people have used telescopes to see faraway things.

Modern telescopes are bigger and better than ever before — and some of them have been sent into space for a better look.

On December 25th 2021, the **James Webb Space Telescope** was launched into space.

There were no astronauts aboard, so its 18 mirrors were programmed to open out on their own.

It's huge — as long as a tennis court and as tall as a three-floor building — and it can see a type of light humans can't, called **infrared**.

When light from a star travels a really, **really** long way, it becomes infrared.

Being able to see infrared means the James Webb Telescope can see far-off galaxies — and look through clouds of dust, too.

WITHOUT INFRARED

WITH INFRARED

Scientists know the most distant galaxies from Earth are the very oldest. Stars here are around **13 billion** years old.

By seeing the light of these ancient stars, the James Webb Telescope is actually looking back in time — almost as far as the **beginning of the universe**.

When a star stops shining...

A star shines brightly for a very long time — for a few millon or even billion years. But one day every star will stop shining and change. What happens next?

There are all kinds of stars. But some of the biggest stars grow bigger and bigger, swallowing everything around them until...

...their insides collapse and their outsides...

...EXPLODE!!!!!

This is a **supernova**.

What's left behind is called a **neutron star**.

A neutron star is VERY tightly packed. If it were the size of a sugar cube on Earth, it would weigh as much as a mountain.

When a star becomes a hole...

Sometimes a star is so huge, at the end of its life, something different happens...

It collapses so much, it turns inside out and makes a hole in space!

It's called a **black hole**!

Wahaha help!

A black hole has stronger gravity than **anything else** in the universe. So, anything that gets too close to a black hole is pulled inside – even light.

It's impossible to **see** a black hole. But what astronomers **have** seen is glowing stars whizzing around one like water vanishing down a plug hole. In 2022, for the first time ever, they took a picture of this happening around the **supermassive** black hole in the middle of the Milky Way.

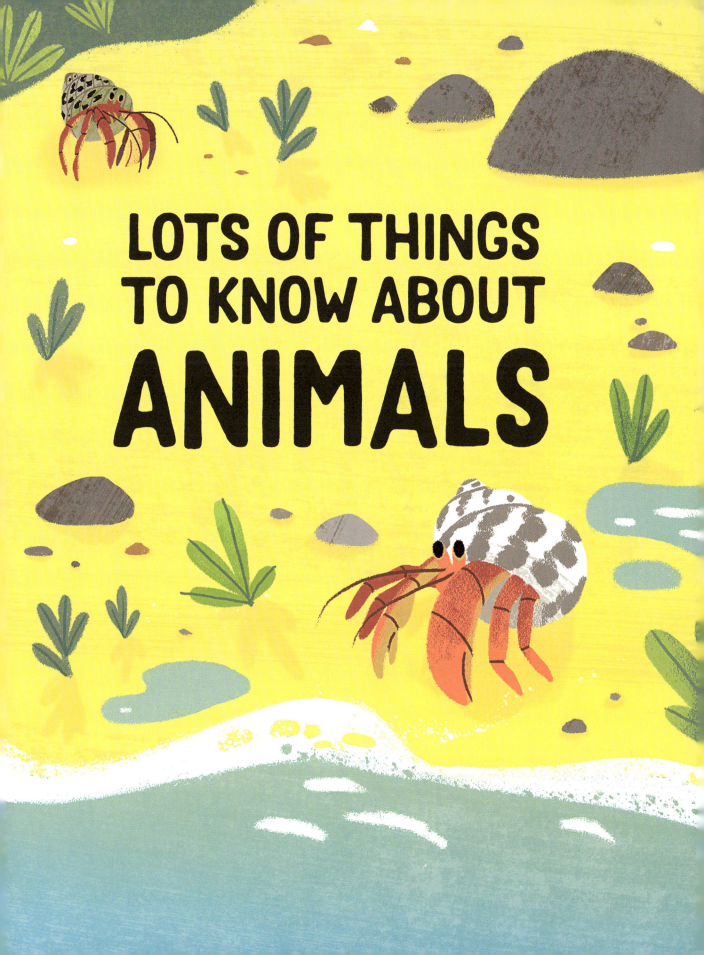

LOTS OF THINGS TO KNOW ABOUT
ANIMALS

Ocean giants

Of all the creatures that have ever lived on Earth, blue whales are the largest. But how **big** are their body parts?

A blue whale's tail is as wide as a football net.

Its heart is as big as a bumper car.

The baby animal that's LARGER than its parents

Almost all animals are much, much **bigger** than their babies.

Check the number under each adult to see how much heavier it is than its newborn baby.

LLAMA

10 TIMES

PYTHON

20 TIMES

SNOWY OWL

40 TIMES

Snowy owl chicks are similar in size to small oranges.

But there are frogs in the Amazon Rainforest, called paradoxical frogs, whose babies aren't so small...

The frogs lay eggs that hatch into tadpoles, which grow almost **four times** bigger than the adult frogs.

GIANT PANDA

A newborn panda weighs about the same as an apple.

It takes at least 30 years for sea turtles to become fully grown.

LOGGERHEAD SEA TURTLE

LEOPARD

900 TIMES

6,750 TIMES

Baby leopard cubs are six times smaller than adult pet cats.

80 TIMES

You're such a BIG baby!

As they grow up, paradoxical frog tadpoles sprout legs, lose their tails and **shrink**.

How to spot a leopard...   ...from a jaguar

Leopards and jaguars are types of big cats with big, splotchy spots. To tell them apart, you just need to examine their markings...

Both leopards and jaguars have splotches shaped like flowers. They are called **rosettes**.

LEOPARD

JAGUAR

But only the rosettes on a jaguar's fur have little spots inside them.

Why horses dress up like zebras

Some animals are less likely to suffer insect bites than others. For instance, zebras...

Their stripes **dazzle** flies, so they can't see where to land and bite.

BZZZ

OUCH!

It's much easier for flies to attack horses...

...**unless** they're wearing a rug.

BZZZ

You can't bite us.

And the **best** rugs for stopping flies have black and white stripes.

Octopuses in disguise

Most octopuses can change the way their skin looks to match the ocean floor.

This helps them to hide from sharks and other hunters...

...as well as the sea creatures that they try to hunt.

Common octopuses sometimes cover their bodies with seashells to keep out of sight.

Veined octopuses carry two coconut halves...

...so they can hide inside them.

HAVE YOU SEEN THIS OCTOPUS?

It's a mimic octopus. This type of octopus scares away hunters by **pretending** to be poisonous animals.

It can make the shape of a flatfish, called a...

BANDED SOLE

It fans out its arms to match the spines of a...

LIONFISH

It wiggles just two arms and hides the rest of its body beneath the sand, so it looks like this snake.

SEA KRAIT

137

How tiny ants are actually STRONGER than gorillas

To find out which animals are stronger than which, you could compare how much they **weigh** with how much they can **carry**...

Gorillas are strong enough to lift **four** times their own weight.

Tigers use their powerful jaws to drag cows **twice** as heavy as themselves.

Harpy eagles are strong enough to snatch monkeys that weigh the **same** as them.

The muscles in gorillas' arms are bigger than in their legs. That's what makes them such great weightlifters.

WORLD'S STRONGEST ANIMAL COMPETITION

But some of the smallest animals on Earth can carry **even more**.

Leafcutter ants pick up pieces of leaves that each weigh as much as **20** ants.

They carry the pieces to their nests.

20 TIMES

50 TIMES

And there are dung beetles that can roll balls of poo **50** times heavier than their own body weight.

Dung beetles collect animals' poo to eat and lay their eggs in.

I can't even lift half my body weight.

How HIGH can birds and bumblebees fly?

Scientists have proved that bumblebees can fly higher than the peak of Mount Everest – the **highest** mountain in the world.

HEIGHT: 8,849m (29,032ft)

BUZZZZ

BUZZZZ

When you hear bees buzz, you're actually listening to their wings flap – 200 times every second.

BUZZZ

The highest-flying birds are Rüppell's vultures. They can soar at heights of 11,300m (37,000ft).

That's as high up as a plane.

How LOW can sea creatures go?

Enormous cracks in the ocean floor, called trenches, are the deepest places on Earth. They're **pitch black** and **freezing cold**, but some animals live inside them...

This scary-looking creature is an anglerfish. It has a spine dangling from the front of its head that glows in the dark. Little fish are attracted to the light, and the anglerfish gobbles them up.

Snailfish swim **deeper** than any other types of fish. They have soft, jelly-like bodies.

And even at the bottom of the very deepest trenches, there are tube-shaped creatures called sea cucumbers.

The secret of hornbills' nests

Hornbills are strange-looking birds with unusually big beaks. Even more bizarre are the steps they take to lay their eggs...

First, a mother hornbill finds a tree with a large hole in its trunk.

The father brings mud to the hole.

Together, they build a wall that traps the mother inside for **months**.

Here are some more animals with **amazing** nests...

Mother alligators make nests out of rotting plants.

The eggs in the **warmer** parts of the nest hatch into males...

...and the eggs in **cooler** parts hatch into females.

Don't worry! There's a slit in the mud wall so the father can pass the mother things to eat.

Safe in the nest, the mother lays her eggs and waits for them to hatch.

There's a nest on a cliff in Greenland that birds called gyrfalcons have used for more than 2,500 years.

My great, great, great, great, great, great granny hatched up here.

Paradise fish blow lots of tiny **bubbles** to make nests that float.

Incredible!

The great shell swap

Most crabs have a hard shell around a soft body, but hermit crabs are a little different. Because they can't grow shells, every hermit crab has to find an old seashell to live inside instead.

Can you guess what happens when they get too big for their shells?

It's feeling tight in here. Time to find a bigger shell...

When an empty shell washes up on a beach, hermit crabs arrive to check it out...

If the shell looks **too big**, they line up in order of size and **wait**.

What are you all doing?

They're waiting for a BIGGER crab to come along. HERE'S one now!

At last a hermit crab the right fit for the new shell will crawl into it. The crab leaves its old shell for the next in line.

The perfect home!

And then each crab changes its shell for the one in front — until there's one little shell left empty at the end of the line.

Noisy animals you CAN'T hear

Many animals aren't as quiet as they seem. They make sounds that are either **too high** or **too low** for people to hear, such as...

Elephants' low, rumbling sounds travel a long way, even in thick, leafy forests.

Some rats laugh at a very high pitch when they're tickled.

PLAYLIST: FOR ANIMALS' EARS ONLY

RUMBLES
African forest elephants

GIGGLES
Rats

CLICKS
Sperm whales

CHIRPS
Torrent frogs

Noisier than planes at take-off, sperm whales are the loudest animals in the world. Luckily for your ears, the clicks they make are far too low for humans to hear.

These frogs' chirps are high enough for them to hear each other over the loud waterfalls where they live.

I can't hear anything!

That's because these sounds are too high or too low for us.

146

Treetop choirs

The biggest — and **noisiest** — lemurs on the island of Madagascar are called indris. Every day, groups of them sing from the treetops where they live.

The oldest female and male in each group start a duet. They make high and low notes to the same beat.

EEEYA... EEEEYA...

EEEYA... EEEEYA...

EEEYA...

Then, other members of their family join in with the song.

EEEYA...

But there comes a time when a young male indri sings **out of tune**.

OHHHHHHHH

He does this when he's ready to leave the group and start his own family.

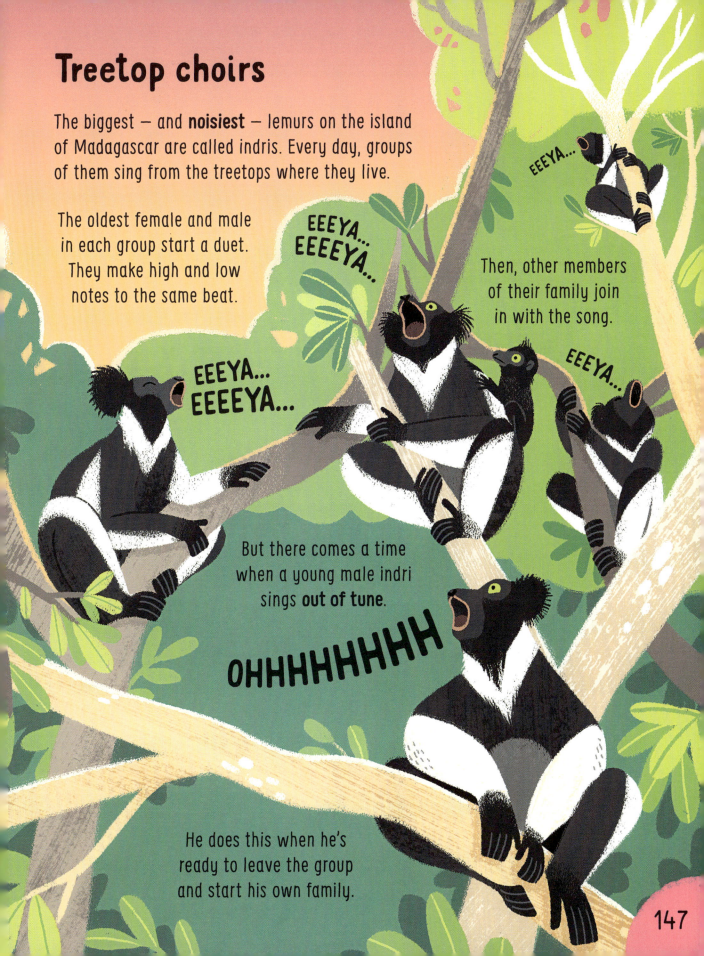

The cave of bats that's busier than New York

Every summer, lots and lots of bats fly from Mexico to Texas, USA, to have their babies in Bracken Cave.

The bats rest inside during the day. But the adults fly out at night to catch insects.

As the babies grow up, they join the hunt too. This swells the swarm to more than **15 million** bats.

There are twice as many bats in Bracken Cave as there are people in New York – the largest city in America.

Where do the bats go in winter?

They fly back to Mexico, where it's warmer.

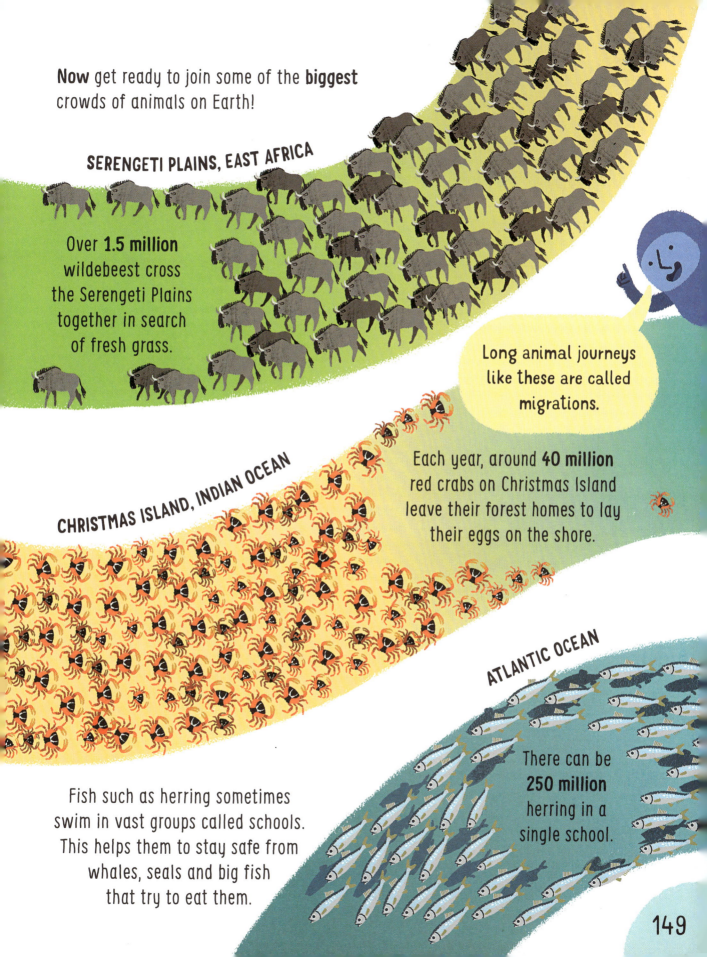

Now get ready to join some of the **biggest** crowds of animals on Earth!

SERENGETI PLAINS, EAST AFRICA

Over **1.5 million** wildebeest cross the Serengeti Plains together in search of fresh grass.

Long animal journeys like these are called **migrations**.

Each year, around **40 million** red crabs on Christmas Island leave their forest homes to lay their eggs on the shore.

CHRISTMAS ISLAND, INDIAN OCEAN

ATLANTIC OCEAN

There can be **250 million** herring in a single school.

Fish such as herring sometimes swim in vast groups called schools. This helps them to stay safe from whales, seals and big fish that try to eat them.

149

You'll hardly BELIEVE your eyes!

These animals could all steal the show with the **amazing** things they do to impress, confuse or scare each other.

 **HOODED SEAL**

That's not a red balloon! This is what a male hooded seal looks like when he blows up his inflatable nose.

This strange-looking creature can roll into a near perfect ball. It tucks in its legs and slots its nose snugly beside its tail.

 **THREE-BANDED ARMADILLO**

 **SUPERB BIRD-OF-PARADISE**

When this type of bird fans out its feathers, it makes a weird black and turquoise shape that doesn't look like a bird at all.

Springboks are the bounciest show-offs. They leap three times their own height...

...and keep their legs straight.

SPRINGBOK

To startle an attacker, this lizard flips up dazzling flaps of skin around its head.

FRILLED LIZARD

KILLDEER

Why is it pretending to be injured?

This bird seems to have a broken wing... but it's **faking** it.

So hunters try to catch the bird INSTEAD of spotting its babies.

Which live LONGEST?

If you look at the candles on these birthday cakes, you'll find out the record-breaking ages of some of the world's oldest animals.

Happy birthday to you...

185 GIANT TORTOISE

100 COCKATOO

400 GREENLAND SHARK

200 BOWHEAD WHALE

500 OCEAN QUAHOG CLAM

Animals from dinosaur times

The last dinosaurs died a long, long time ago. But a few of the types of creatures that lived alongside them are still around **now**...

DRAGONFLY

MOSQUITO

BEE

COCKROACH

When scientists tested the bones of a T. rex...

...they discovered that **chickens** are some of its closest living relatives.

MILLIPEDE

ANT

153

Why whales blow bubbles

Blowing bubbles can be surprisingly **useful** for groups of humpback whales.

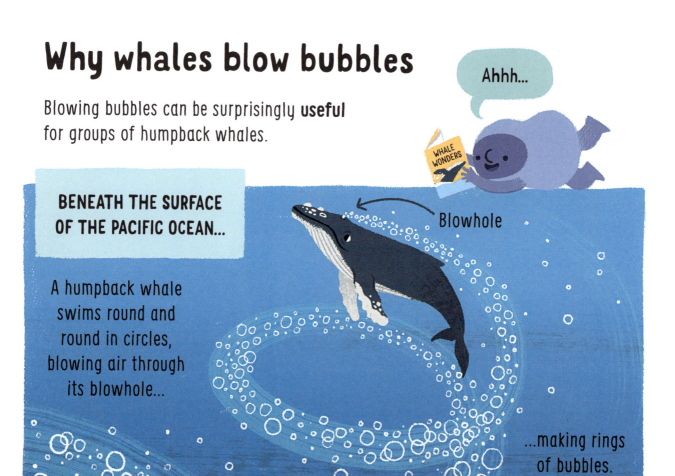

BENEATH THE SURFACE OF THE PACIFIC OCEAN...

A humpback whale swims round and round in circles, blowing air through its blowhole...

Blowhole

...making rings of bubbles.

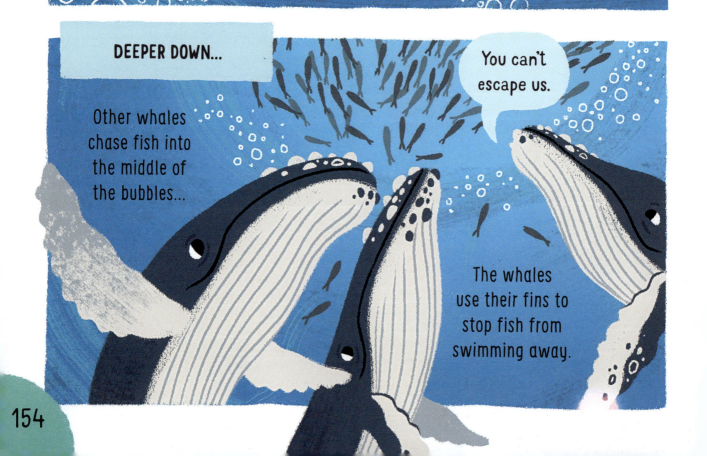

DEEPER DOWN...

Other whales chase fish into the middle of the bubbles...

The whales use their fins to stop fish from swimming away.

Suddenly, one of the whales makes a noise:

WHIIIIEEOOOO

It's a signal for all of them to swim up.

Then they open their mouths wide, and...

...eat.

So that's why whales blow bubbles: to make fishing nets.

155

How do prairie dogs say hello?

Prairie dogs are **not** dogs. They're small, furry animals that live together in burrows. But they do bark to warn of danger, and when they meet a prairie dog they know...

Lions **rub** their heads together.

EEEEEEEEE

EEEEE EEEEEE

Dolphins **whistle**.

Lobsters squirt **wee** at one another from holes in their heads.

A young fox **crouches** low and folds back its ears to greet an adult fox.

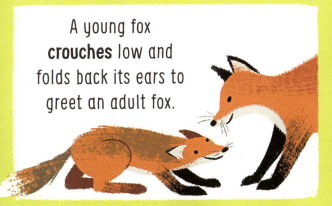

Elephants **touch** trunks.

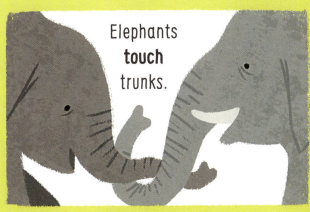

Chimpanzees share a **hug**.

Dogs **sniff** bottoms. The smells remind them if they've met before.

157

Why sloths turn green in the rain

Sloths are slow, sleepy creatures. But their shaggy fur is **crawling** with all kinds of living things...

LICE

MOSQUITOS

TICKS

MOTHS

ALGAE

Tiny plants called algae grow in the fur, too. When it rains, the algae turn green — and so does the sloth.

Looking green is a good thing for sloths. It helps them to hide up in the trees.

What makes flamingos pink

When they first hatch out, flamingos are a dull grey.

Their feathers and skin start to turn pink when they eat brine shrimp living in water.

BRINE SHRIMP

The more shrimp flamingos eat, the **pinker** they become.

SHADES OF FLAMINGO

| JUST HATCHED | FLUFFY CLOUD | FIRST FLUSH |

| PINKING | BLUSH | IN THE PINK |

PINKEST

What's that flamingo doing?

It's rubbing oil from the base of its tail onto its feathers. This turns them even pinker.

What's for dinner?

Can you imagine a restaurant where animals could eat?
There'd be some very strange things on the menu...

Blood

You might have heard that vampire bats
bite animals to drink their blood, but did
you know that there are also vampire moths?

Soil

Soil contains salt, which
animals need to keep healthy.

Turtle tears

Tears are salty, too. In the
Amazon Rainforest, butterflies land
on turtles to drink from their eyes.

Chef says
we've run out
of soil!

That's because so many
animals eat it: parrots,
orangutans, elephants, sheep...

Poisonous leaves

The leaves on eucalyptus trees are poisonous for most animals — except koalas. Their stomachs can break down the poisons safely.

Old skin

Lizards shed their skin. Sometimes, they swallow the pieces they tear off.

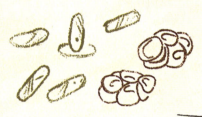

Fresh poo

Guinea pigs and rabbits eat any soft poos that they do because they still contain stuff that's good for them.

Half-eaten meat

Wolves bring up food from their tummies for young wolves. This makes it soft enough for them to eat.

Animal life in a land of ice

Brrrr! Even in summer, many parts of the Antarctic are chillier than a kitchen freezer. So how do the animals here stay alive and warm?

EMPEROR PENGUINS

Penguins have layers of different feathers.

Stiff feathers on top are waterproof.

Fluffy feathers close to their skin trap heat.

ADÉLIE PENGUINS

Emperor penguins rock back on the heels of their feet to stop their toes from freezing in the snow.

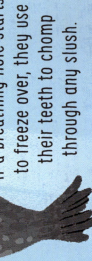

When they need to pop up for air, they find holes in the ice.

If a breathing hole starts to freeze over, they use their teeth to chomp through any slush.

WEDDELL SEAL

Seals spend as many as nine out of every ten hours swimming under the ice.

The animal that would win a marathon

A marathon is a running race over 42km (26 miles) long.

Cheetahs reach the fastest speeds of any animals on land, but they can't keep going over long distances — so they'd be no good in marathons.

Horses can run fast and far. They'd finish a marathon in two and a half hours. That's as fast as the best human athletes.

Camels are even better marathon runners than horses.

I'd reach the finish line after one hour only.

And thanks to their long, powerful legs, ostriches would be the **winners**.

Finish time:

45 MINUTES

SURPRISING swimmers

The animals on this page spend most of their lives on the ground or up trees, but they're all impressively strong swimmers too.

TIGERS
Unlike many other types of cats, tigers enjoy getting wet.

ELEPHANTS

> I use my trunk as a snorkel to breathe.

SLOTHS
Sloths are three times faster in water than on land.

PIGS
Pigs can swim long distances to cross rivers.

The animals' tool kit

Did you know that some animals are so clever that they've learned how to use tools?

Check out what's inside their tool kit on these pages.

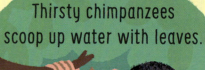
Thirsty chimpanzees scoop up water with leaves.

STICKS

LEAVES

If a puffin has an itch, it picks up a stick to scratch itself.

Monkeys called long-tailed macaques clean their teeth with feathers.

FEATHERS

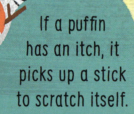

TOP TOOLS FOR ANIMALS

Asian elephants hold branches in their trunks and swing them to swat bothersome flies.

Woodpecker finches use spines from spiky cactus plants to prise tasty insects out from cracks.

Natural sponges grow on the sea floor.

Some dolphins pluck them to wear on their noses so they can dig for fish in rocky sand without getting scratched.

Capuchin monkeys smash nuts out of their shells by hammering them with big stones.

BRANCHES

CACTUS SPINES

SPONGES

STONES

167

You'll never guess why pandas do handstands...

You may want to pinch your nose, because things are about to get very, very **smelly**...

Pandas use all kinds of smells to send messages to each other and show where they live.

They leave piles of dung for other pandas to sniff.

Aha – a female panda lives nearby.

They make smells under their tails and rub them onto rocks and trees.

And male pandas have found another way to spread their smells around too.

They stand on their front paws next to a tree...

...and spray their strong-smelling wee high up its trunk.

This tells other male pandas to STAY AWAY.

...and what shape poos wombats do

If you think animal poo is yucky, **look away now.**

ELEPHANT

A ball of elephant dung is about the size of a cauliflower.

 WOMBAT

Wombats' poos are unlike any other animal's — they're cube-shaped.

BLUE WHALE

Blue whale poo is bright orange, and just one blue whale poo would fill about 20 buckets.

 PARROTFISH

Parrotfish grind rock-like coral into tiny pieces when they eat. So, when they poo, sand comes out.

 HIPPO

Hippos spin their tails to spray their dung far and wide.

Animal architects

Small animals make great builders, when it comes to designing and constructing places to live.

SOCIABLE WEAVERS

Sociable weavers are birds that live in groups of 200 or more. They collect grass to make one **giant nest** for their group.

Lots of entrance tunnels lead to different parts of the nest.

The middle of the nest stays warm when it's cold at night.

GREEN ANTS

Adult

Baby

Silk

Green ants join leaves together to build nests. For glue, they use **sticky** silk made by their babies.

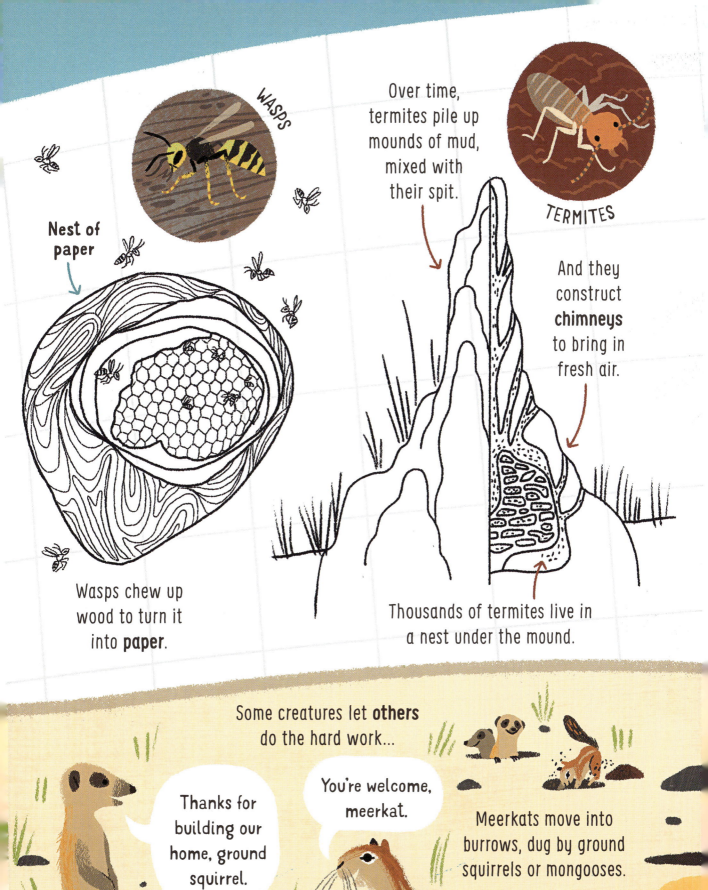

WASPS

TERMITES

Over time, termites pile up mounds of mud, mixed with their spit.

And they construct **chimneys** to bring in fresh air.

Nest of paper

Wasps chew up wood to turn it into **paper**.

Thousands of termites live in a nest under the mound.

Some creatures let **others** do the hard work...

Thanks for building our home, ground squirrel.

You're welcome, meerkat.

Meerkats move into burrows, dug by ground squirrels or mongooses.

Walking on water

Lizards mostly live on land, but there are a few types that can do some amazing things in water.

This basilisk lizard can run across rivers without **sinking**.

Flaps of skin between its toes keep it afloat.

Marine iguanas are the only lizards that live in the sea.

After swimming, they get rid of salty seawater from their bodies by sneezing.

oooooooooooooooooo

Aaachoooooooooooooo

Little lizards called water anoles blow bubbles that stick to their heads.

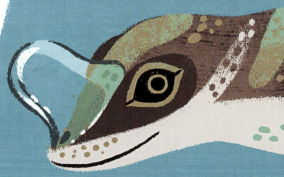

This gives them air to breathe underwater for over 15 minutes.

Snakes in the air

Snakes don't have wings, but some can appear to **fly** between trees. They are called flying snakes.

First, a flying snake pushes itself off a branch.

Then, it wiggles its body and makes itself flat to **glide** through the air.

Hey! All of these different animals can glide too...

Yes, and spiders shoot silk threads to catch a breeze, which carries them through the air.

FLYING SQUIRREL

GLIDING FROG

FLYING SQUID

Whodunit

Beware thieves!
The animals in this line-up
are all known to **steal**...

Spotted hyenas do hunt for themselves, but sometimes they snatch food from wild dogs.

SPOTTED HYENA

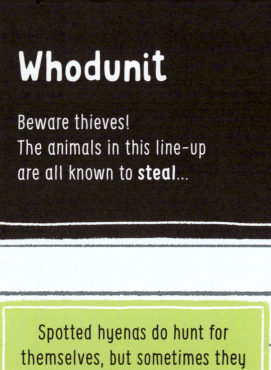

LION

Adult male lions work alone. A single lion can steal food from a gang of hyenas all for himself.

How baby swifts get ready to cross continents

At the start of summer, swifts fly from Africa to parts of Asia and Europe. When they get there, they make nests in cracks and crevices where they lay their eggs.

After hatching, swift chicks only have one or two months to grow up. Then it's time to leave their nest and go on the **extraordinarily long** journey to Africa **non-stop**.

Are their wings strong enough to fly such a long way?

Yes! They practise with press-ups inside the nest.

The birds that fly further than astronauts

Of all the birds on Earth, Arctic terns fly **furthest**.

ARCTIC TERN

ARCTIC

ANTARCTIC

Every year, as summer ends in the Arctic, they fly to the Antarctic – where summer is just beginning. And when summer ends there, they fly **back!**

Arctic terns make this incredible journey because they need bright, sunny days to hunt fish.

In its lifetime, an Arctic tern can fly more than 2.4 million km (1.5 million miles) – that's about the same as three trips to and from the Moon.

Old and new body parts

Lots of animals lose hairs, scales, teeth, claws and other parts of their bodies throughout their lives. But often they grow back.

Sharks have hundreds of teeth in rows. Whenever a tooth drops out, it's replaced by the one growing behind it.

As they get older, snakes, crabs and spiders shed the outer layer of their bodies in **one piece**.

Every year, the antlers on male deer's heads fall off.

In its lifetime, a single shark can grow as many as **30,000** teeth.

Each male starts growing a new pair just a few weeks later.

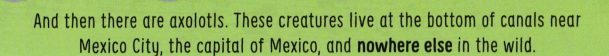

And then there are axolotls. These creatures live at the bottom of canals near Mexico City, the capital of Mexico, and **nowhere else** in the wild.

Those frilly parts behind an axolotl's head help it to breathe. They're called gills.

Big fish live here, too, and sometimes, while trying to catch an axolotl, they bite one of its legs right off.

Uh oh...

But the whole leg will grow back — toes and all.

It can take several weeks or months for an axolotl to regrow all the skin, muscles and bones that make up its leg.

First aid for orangutans

Orangutans live in trees, but climbing up trunks, swinging between branches and carrying young orangutans can make their arms **ache**. They can't visit a doctor — so what do they do?

OUCH...

OW

Orangutans search for a type of plant that they **never** eat.

But they chew its leaves to make a foamy lotion...

...which they spit out and rub into sore parts of their bodies.

What's so good about these leaves?

They contain chemicals that SOOTHE pain.

FIRST AID

KEEP BACK!

These three animals have one thing in common — they all use a type of poison called **venom**.

A stingray is a type of fish. It whips its tail to inject venom through a long spine.

STINGRAY

PLATYPUS

Male platypuses have spikes on their back legs to sting with venom.

SPITTING COBRA

Some snakes shoot venom from their fangs.

DON'T TOUCH!

This bird's feathers and this frog's skin are both covered in poison.

WARNING
HOODED PITOHUI

Scientists think that their poison comes from all the poisonous beetles and ants that they eat.

DANGER
GOLDEN DART FROG

If they stopped eating these insects, they would become **less poisonous**.

How animals make art

The starburst design inside this frame is as pretty as a painting. But the artists who create these patterns live under the sea.

Patterns like this are made in the sandy sea floor, near Japan, by male white-spotted pufferfish.

It takes each fish about a week to create his work of art. He shapes the sand with his fins and clears away any untidy stones with his mouth.

WHITE-SPOTTED PUFFERFISH

Why do the male pufferfish go to all that effort?

To impress females, so they can have babies together.

Male bowerbirds also take great care to get the attention of females. They arrange sticks into intricate structures, called **bowers**.

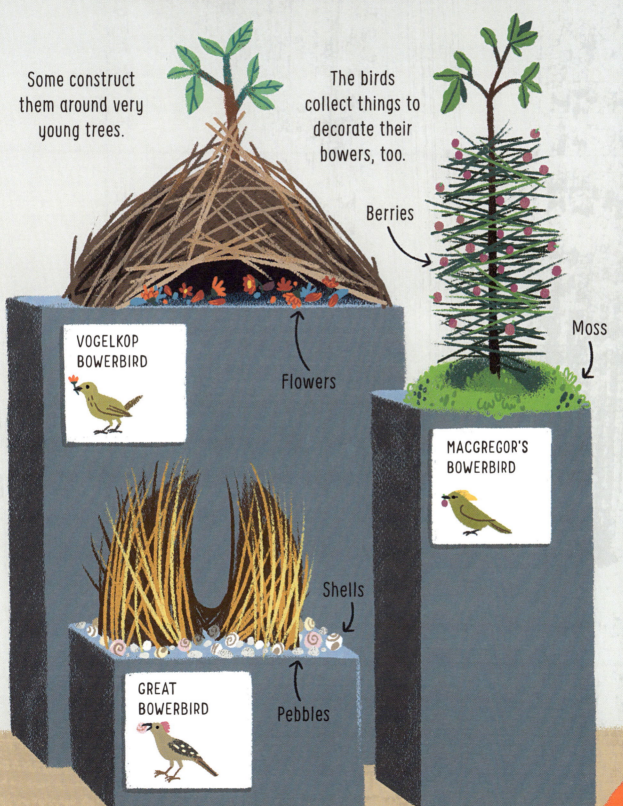

Some construct them around very young trees.

The birds collect things to decorate their bowers, too.

Berries

Moss

VOGELKOP BOWERBIRD

Flowers

MACGREGOR'S BOWERBIRD

Shells

GREAT BOWERBIRD

Pebbles

Whose bones?

If you could look inside different animals with the help of a giant X-ray machine, you'd see pictures like these...

Find the two tall bumps on top of this giraffe's skull. They're called **ossicones**.

There are seven bones in a giraffe's neck. That's the same number as you have in yours.

Snakes' skeletons are mostly made up of just two kinds of bones — but they can have **hundreds** of each.

VERTEBRAE ←

RIBS ←

Beavers' tails are wide and flat to help them to steer while swimming. But there's only a thin row of bones through the middle.

(Giraffe neck bones are much, much *longer* than human ones of course.)

It's the only one on these pages that's ACTUAL SIZE! This type of narrow-mouthed frog has one of the smallest skeletons in the world.

What about this tiny X-ray?

An elephant's trunk disappears on X-rays because it's **boneless.**

This is a bat's thumb bone.

The four spindly bones that stretch to the tips of the wing are fingers.

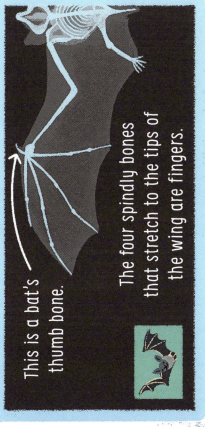

Is it a bird? No — it's the skull of a blue whale.

Polar bear names

Polar bears are called **polar** bears because they live on sea ice near the North **Pole**. But there are other words for this creature from around the world and long ago...

Nanuk

White sea deer

Old man in the fur cloak

White bear

Rider of icebergs

Ice bear

Ursus maritimus

Err... What does *Ursus maritimus* mean?

That's its scientific name. It's made up of the words for BEAR and SEA in a language called Latin.

Celebrity animals

Several kinds of animals are named after famous people. Look closely at the scientific names and find out who's who.

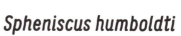

Spheniscus humboldti

German explorer Alexander von Humboldt

Please may I have your autograph?

Zaglossus attenboroughi

British TV presenter David Attenborough

Humboldt penguins live on the west coast of South America.

This is a type of echidna. It has a long snout and lives in New Guinea.

Stasimopus mandelai

South African leader Nelson Mandela

This type of spider is found in South Africa.

Scaptia beyonceae

American singer Beyoncé

This Australian horse fly has golden hairs at the tip of its body.

Craspedotropis gretathunbergae

Swedish campaigner Greta Thunberg

Scientists discovered this tiny snail in the forests of Brunei.

Why sleeping sea otters sometimes hold paws

Sea otters spend almost all their time in water – even when they're asleep.

Before going to sleep, a sea otter wraps itself in kelp plants so it won't float away.

And pairs of otters hold paws to make sure they don't **drift apart**.

Kelp is a type of large seaweed that grows up from the ocean floor.

Shhh! These animals are all fast asleep too...

After a big meal, Komodo dragons — the largest lizards in the world — sleep for as much as a **whole week**.

That's 168 hours.

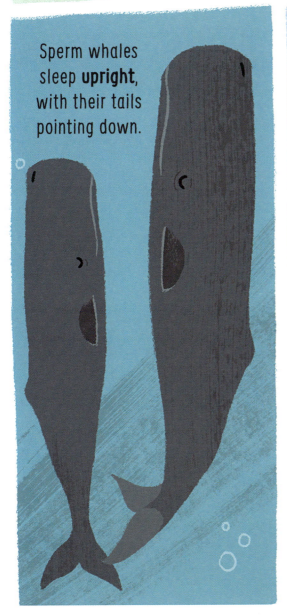

Sperm whales sleep **upright**, with their tails pointing down.

Sea birds called great frigatebirds can sleep while **gliding** in mid-air.

Giraffes, zebras and elephants can all sleep and stay **standing up**.

189

LOTS OF THINGS TO KNOW ABOUT
DINOSAURS

New dinosaurs

Did you know that scientists keep discovering new types of dinosaurs each year?

The fossil of a dinosaur called Changmiania was found recently in China.

Um, what's a FOSSIL?

Fossils are rock-like remains left behind by dinosaurs, other animals and plants.

CHANGMIANIA

Long, long, long, long, long, LONG ago

To help you to imagine just how far back you'd need to go to meet **living** dinosaurs, follow this line as it spirals down the page...

NOW

ANCIENT EGYPT
4,500 YEARS AGO

CAVE PAINTINGS
20,000 YEARS AGO

WOOLLY MAMMOTHS
300,000 YEARS AGO

Dinosaurs? I've never seen one. You still need to go 250 times further back in time.

1 MILLION YEARS AGO

10 MILLION YEARS AGO

30 MILLION YEARS AGO

DINOSAURS
BETWEEN 66 AND 250 MILLION YEARS AGO

Hello. You've reached us at last.

Dinosaur times

Even if you've seen it on television or in a film, Stegosaurus never met Triceratops — and Tyrannosaurus rex never chased Diplodocus! That's because dinosaurs didn't all live at the same time. Some were separated from each other by **millions** and **millions** of years.

You can see the **whole** time that dinosaurs were around on the pages of this unusual calendar...

Dinosaur times are divided into three stages: Triassic, Jurassic and Cretaceous.

Aha!

TRIASSIC

The **first** dinosaurs were quite small. They all walked on two legs.

EORAPTOR

INGENTIA

250 MYA

200 MYA

By the end of the Triassic, there were bigger dinosaurs that started to walk on four legs.

MYA stands for MILLION YEARS AGO.

JURASSIC

DIPLODOCUS

For a long, long time, there were only trees and leafy ferns for plant-eating dinosaurs.

200 MYA

STEGOSAURUS

150 MYA

CRETACEOUS

IGUANODON

Then, later on, the first flowers bloomed.

150 MYA

100 MYA

TYRANNOSAURUS REX

And when the last dinosaurs arrived there were ants, bees and butterflies, too.

TRICERATOPS

100 MYA

66 MYA

What dinosaurs ACTUALLY looked like

The **fossils** left by dinosaurs don't always show the whole picture, but they give lots of clues. They show...

...the shapes of their bodies

...the lengths of their claws

...how many teeth they had

...and that some dinosaurs were covered in feathers.

But all the **colours** in the dinosaur pictures on this page are total guesses.

No one really knows which dinosaurs were red, yellow, pink, green, purple, brown or blue — except for a very few types. Such as, Psittacosaurus...

Scientists found enough **skin** in a fossil of this dinosaur to work out its colours and patterns.

PSITTACOSAURUS FOSSIL

PSITTACOSAURUS

What are those yellow spikes on its tail?

They were found in the fossil too. They're called bristles.

Dinosaurs the size of rabbits

Did you know that **some** dinosaurs were **small** enough to hold in your arms?
To understand just how little they could be, you could compare
them with more familiar animals...

EPIDEXIPTERYX

SQUIRREL

MICRORAPTOR

PIGEON

HALSZKARAPTOR

HESPERONYCHUS

CAT

DUCK

MEI

How much bigger were the BIGGEST dinosaurs?

Hundreds of times longer and thousands of times heavier! We'll meet the giants on pages 206-207.

TURKEY

RABBIT

AQUILOPS

What's the point of a dinosaur's tail?

Every single type of dinosaur had a **tail**.

Some tails were very, very, **very** long.

Apatosaurus had a long body and a long neck — but its tail was even longer.

Most of the time, dinosaurs held their tails up in the air. They only left tail tracks on the ground if they crouched down.

DILOPHOSAURUS

One fossil shows marks made in the sand by a Dilophosaurus's tail.

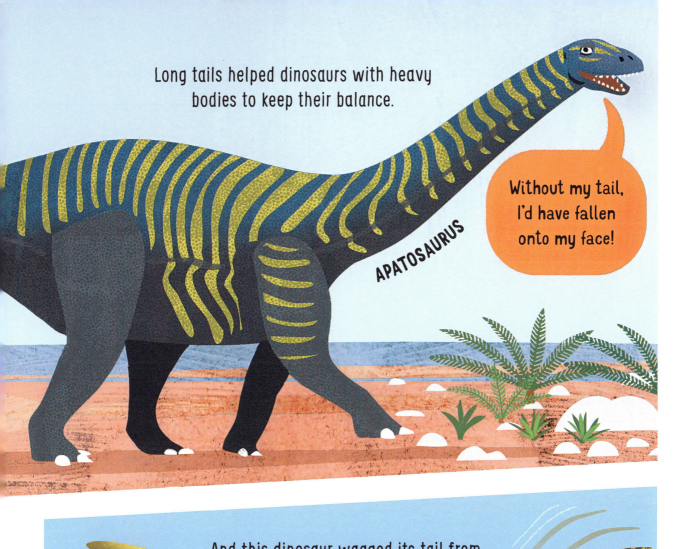

Long tails helped dinosaurs with heavy bodies to keep their balance.

APATOSAURUS

Without my tail, I'd have fallen onto my face!

And this dinosaur wagged its tail from side to side, so it could run **faster**.

COELOPHYSIS

If you don't have a tail, swinging your arms can help you to speed up!

If only I had a tail...

How to tell what dinosaurs ate

You could find out if a dinosaur ate **meat** or **plants** by checking the way it walked.

All the meat-eating dinosaurs walked on **two legs**. They had much smaller arms.

There were plant eaters who used two legs, too, but most of them walked on **four**.

JUICY MEAT

LUSH PLANTS

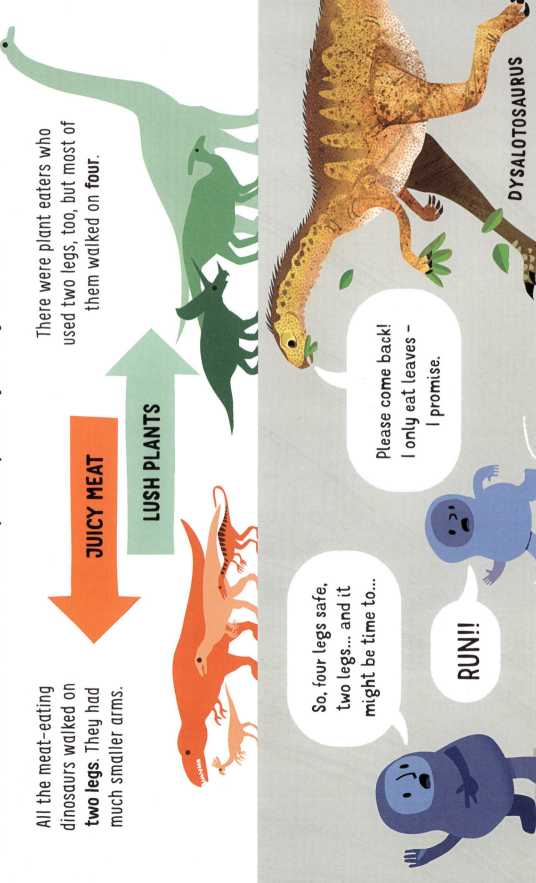

DYSALOTOSAURUS

Please come back! I only eat leaves – I promise.

So, four legs safe, two legs... and it might be time to...

RUN!!

Inside a dinosaur's tummy

If you could go on a journey through a Caudipteryx's body, you'd be surprised when you reached its tummy...

Ouch. Why are there so many stones in here?

Caudipteryx swallowed them to help grind up its food. Sensible, eh?

Dinosaurs in shining armour

So that they didn't end up a meat eater's next meal, these dinosaurs had tough body parts that worked like a suit of armour.

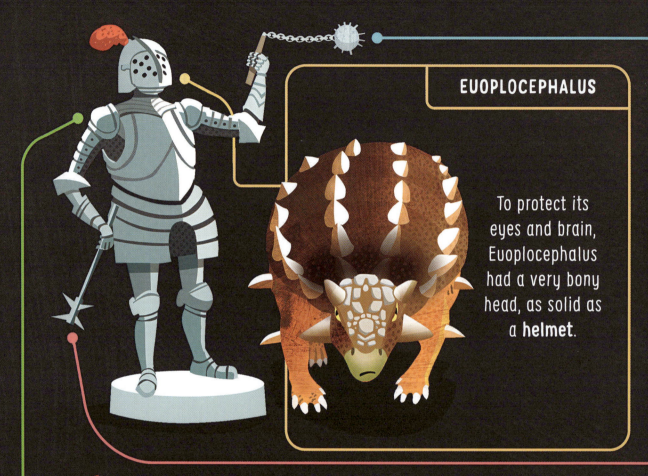

EUOPLOCEPHALUS

To protect its eyes and brain, Euoplocephalus had a very bony head, as solid as a **helmet**.

NODOSAURUS

The **plates** on a Nodosaurus's back were hard and chunky. No dinosaur could bite through them.

ANKYLOSAURUS

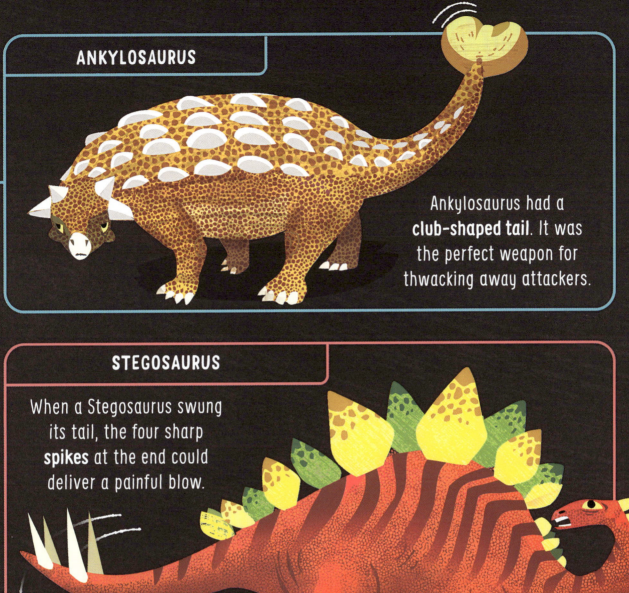

Ankylosaurus had a **club-shaped tail**. It was the perfect weapon for thwacking away attackers.

STEGOSAURUS

When a Stegosaurus swung its tail, the four sharp **spikes** at the end could deliver a painful blow.

SWOOSH

But what about those leaf shapes along its back?

They were too thin to stop dinosaurs from biting them, but they did make Stegosaurus look BIGGER and SCARIER.

The largest creatures ever to walk on Earth

Just one elephant can weigh as much as 60 people. But if you think that sounds heavy, you should take a look at these dinosaurs. They belong to a group of large dinosaurs called **sauropods**.

Even the very smallest sauropods were the same size as elephants.

WEIGHT OF SAUROPODS IN ELEPHANTS

1 ELEPHANT

SALTASAURUS

And the **biggest** sauropods, such as Argentinosaurus, could grow so heavy that they'd outweigh a whole herd of **twelve elephants** — or **720** people.

3 ELEPHANTS

6 ELEPHANTS

10 ELEPHANTS

DIPLODOCUS

GIRAFFATITAN

DREADNOUGHTUS

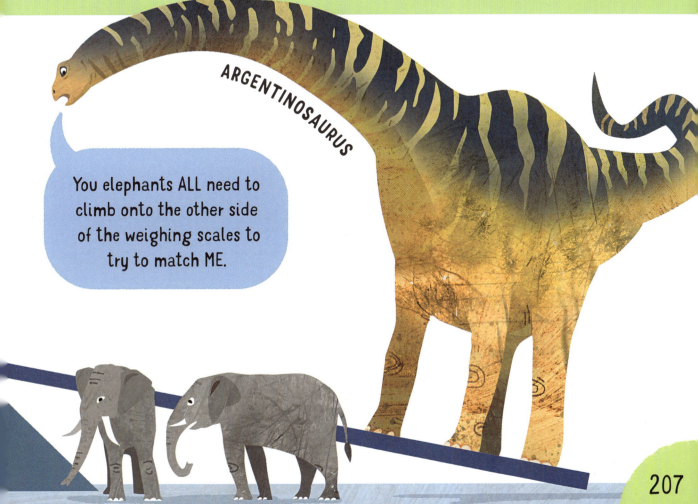

ARGENTINOSAURUS

You elephants ALL need to climb onto the other side of the weighing scales to try to match ME.

The island of Tyrannosaurus rex

Scientists guess that there were about 20,000 Tyrannosaurus rexes alive at a time. But just one of these ferocious hunters was enough to terrify other dinosaurs with its...

...amazing eyesight

...thick, muscly *tail*

...bone-crunching teeth

...springy feet

BEWARE OF THE T. REXES!

...and razor-sharp claws.

Luckily for dinosaurs that lived elsewhere, every single Tyrannosaurus rex was trapped on a huge island called Laramidia, which is now part of the USA and Canada.

Tyrannosaurus Sue

There are only 30 or so **real** Tyrannosaurus rex skeletons in museums around the world. A few of these skeletons have nicknames inspired by the people who dug them up...

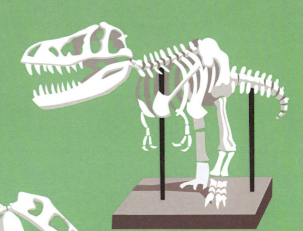

Stan
Stan Sacrison

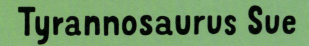

Bucky
Bucky Derflinger

Sue
Sue Hendrickson

Who's Trix?

Trix

It's short for Beatrix. She used to be Queen of the Netherlands – and this skeleton is named after her.

209

The secret sounds of dinosaurs

Did dinosaurs grunt, roar, hiss or squawk? The truth is that there's not much to know for certain about the **noises** they made.

But animals, such as alligators, can help scientists to imagine noisy dinosaurs...

GRRRRRRRR

Like many big animals, alligators make low sounds.

They rumble and grumble while keeping their jaws shut.

Maybe Allosaurus did the same... It was big, too, and alligators are relatives of dinosaurs.

GRRRR

RAH

Raaasss

Hang on... Dinosaurs on TV can be very noisy. WHO made these sounds?

If you ever hear a dinosaur on a computer game or TV show, you're actually listening to lots of different animals.

Crawww

oo ooo aaa aa

Harrgh

Heee-hawwww

sssssssss

Sound designers record their noises and blend them together to make up dinosaur sounds.

TRACK 2: SNARLING T. REX

211

From CHICKEN IMPERSONATOR to WRINKLE FACE

Whenever scientists discover a new type of dinosaur, they have the fun job of making up its **name**. To do this, they often join together words from languages, such as Latin, Ancient Greek and Mandarin Chinese.

Here you'll find the meanings hiding in all these dinosaurs' names...

GALLIMIMUS

CHICKEN IMPERSONATOR

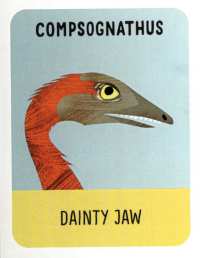

COMPSOGNATHUS

DAINTY JAW

TYLOCEPHALE

LUMP HEAD

MEI

SLEEPY

BARYONYX

HEAVY CLAW

YINLONG

HIDDEN DRAGON

CARNOTAURUS

FLESH BULL

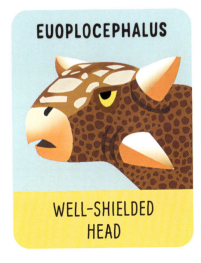

EUOPLOCEPHALUS

WELL-SHIELDED HEAD

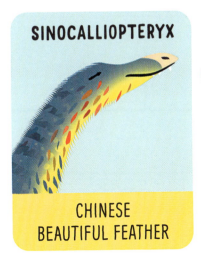

SINOCALLIOPTERYX

CHINESE BEAUTIFUL FEATHER

What a pretty name!

WULONG

DANCING DRAGON

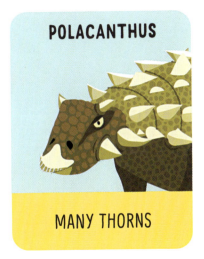

POLACANTHUS

MANY THORNS

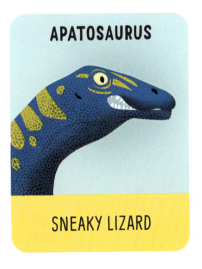

APATOSAURUS

SNEAKY LIZARD

Scientists used to think Oviraptor stole eggs, but now they know it didn't.

OVIRAPTOR

EGG ROBBER

RUGOPS

WRINKLE FACE

In the footsteps of dinosaurs

When dinosaurs stomped across soft mud, they left behind **tracks**.

In hot weather, some muddy tracks dried hard, keeping their shapes.

It hasn't rained one drop since a BIG dinosaur trod here.

Oooooh!

Later, many layers of mud, as well as ash from volcanoes, piled up on top.

Then slowly, so very slowly, the mud underneath turned into **rock**.

And sometimes rocks, just like this one, are unearthed. So **real** dinosaur footprints can still be seen around the world.

Some dinosaur tracks have been found in surprising places.

These tracks used to be flat on the ground...

...but when giant rocks moved below the surface, they forced this rock upwards.

I CAN'T walk up it.

The dinosaurs COULDN'T either.

A trip to the dinosaur dentist

Dentists sometimes take X-rays to examine their patients' **teeth**.
Here's what they'd find in these dinosaurs' mouths...

TYRANNOSAURUS REX

A Tyrannosaurus rex's longest tooth was as **big** as it is in this picture...

ACTUAL SIZE

BRACHIOSAURUS

Brachiosauruses had **gappy** teeth that were shaped like pegs. They were ideal for combing leaves off branches.

SAUROLOPHUS

The back of a Saurolophus's mouth was packed with little teeth in **stacks**. It used them to grind tough pine needles and twigs.

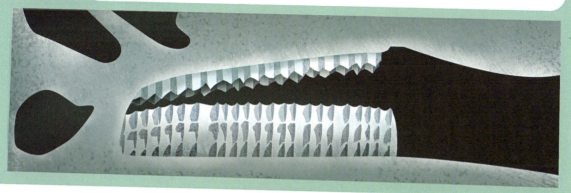

LIMUSAURUS

YOUNG

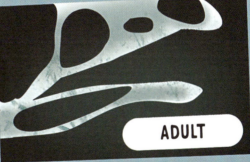

ADULT

What happened to this dinosaur's teeth?

It lost them as it grew up and stopped eating meat. Adult Limusauruses only needed toothless beaks to eat plants.

How ring-shaped nests kept dinosaur eggs safe

All mother dinosaurs laid eggs. They could be smaller than a golf ball or as big as a watermelon. What happened to the eggs before they hatched?

Just like birds, many dinosaurs **sat** on top of their eggs to keep them safe and warm.

CITIPATI

Heavyweight dinosaurs couldn't do this. They'd have crushed the shells!

To make their nests cosy, Edmontosauruses **lined** them with leaves.

EDMONTOSAURUS

SALTASAURUS

Some sauropods **buried** their eggs in hot parts of the ground. Then they left them behind.

But there were giant parents who found a **shatterproof** way to sit on their nests...

GIGANTORAPTOR

Gigantoraptor laid eggs in a ring and sat down in the middle without squashing them.

Oh yes! It's the same shape as my cake.

219

See inside dinosaur eggs

The shells of dinosaur **eggs** were either hard and crisp or soft and leathery. It took several weeks or even months for the babies inside them to grow.

When it was running out of room to get any bigger, this baby oviraptorosaur tucked its head between its legs.

Inside this round egg, the baby curled up into a ball. It had a sharp point at the end of its snout.

It might have tapped the point against the shell to break its way out. Baby birds have something similar on their beaks.

Is it a unicorn?

No – it's a type of sauropod. Shh!

The baby teeth that NEVER chewed

When scientists took a very close look at the fossilized eggs of a dinosaur called **Massospondylus**, they discovered something **surprising**.

As a baby Massospondylus grew inside its egg...

...it formed not just one but **two** sets of tiny teeth in rows.

The baby lost one of the sets before it hatched.

Then it used the teeth that were left to chomp on plants.

Scientists are still trying to figure out what the lost teeth were for.

You'll never guess how the horns on a Triceratops changed

An adult Triceratops had one of the **largest** heads of any dinosaur. To see how it grew, take a look at the pictures on this page.

As a baby, Triceratops had three little bumps for **horns** and a narrow **frill** above its neck.

Then its frill grew wider, and its horns grew bigger.

At first, the two horns above its eyes were straight.

Then they started to curve backwards...

...before bending forwards when it was old.

The dinosaur with a trombone on its head

The head of a **Parasaurolophus** went through a series of extraordinary changes, too.

A young Parasaurolophus had a round lump on top of its head.

As it grew up, the lump began to stretch out...

...into a long **crest**, shaped like a banana.

HAARNK

Inside its crest, there were tubes that joined up with its nose.

Scientists guess they helped it to make honking sounds, just like a musician blowing through the tubes of a trombone.

I wish my nose could do that!

The planet of the dinosaurs

Dinosaurs couldn't read maps, of course, but none would recognize this picture of the world as its home. That's because the shapes of all the land and seas have **changed**.

Here's what the world looked like when different dinosaurs were alive...

EARTH NOW

70 MILLION YEARS AGO

90 MILLION YEARS AGO

That's more like it.

Much better!

PACHYCEPHALOSAURUS

SEGNOSAURUS

200 MILLION YEARS AGO

Why did the land move?

Because enormous pieces of rock under the ground and sea moved very, very slowly. They're still moving now.

Here's my world.

LYCORHINUS

Some parts of the world used to look and feel surprisingly **different**, too. Take Antarctica. Now it's the coldest place on Earth, where ice-loving penguins live.

But if penguins could travel back in time, they'd find dinosaurs living in warm forests on Antarctica instead.

Whoah – no snow!

WELCOME TO ANTARCTICA

120 MILLION YEARS AGO

IGUANODONTIDS

225

Why dinosaur poo ISN'T smelly

When is a rock not a rock? When it's a fossilized dinosaur **poo**! These types of fossils have lost their yucky smell, but they still contain some of the things that dinosaurs ate...

CRUNCHED BONES

ROTTEN WOOD

CRUSHED SNAIL SHELLS

Fossilized poos are called COPROLITES.

No smell at all!

In some coprolites, you can even see tunnels made by dung beetles. These insects eat poo when it's still soft.

Two of the **biggest** coprolites ever found are about the size of a basketball and a rolled-up yoga mat.

A wee mystery...

There's very little to know for certain about dinosaurs' **wee**. Any wee that they did do dried up in the sunshine or soaked into the ground, so it quickly vanished.

But there are a few strange fossils that look like this...

WATCH OUT!

And scientists think that the patterns in them were made when a dinosaur did a wee onto some sand.

The nose that knows

Rivers and river banks were far from safe when **Spinosaurus** was on the prowl. It had the **longest** body of all the meat eaters — and it was one of the only dinosaurs that could **swim**.

To paddle through the water, Spinosaurus waved its wide tail.

Like most animals, it couldn't smell a thing underwater, but its lengthy snout did help it to hunt.

What's this dinosaur searching for?

Fish to eat!

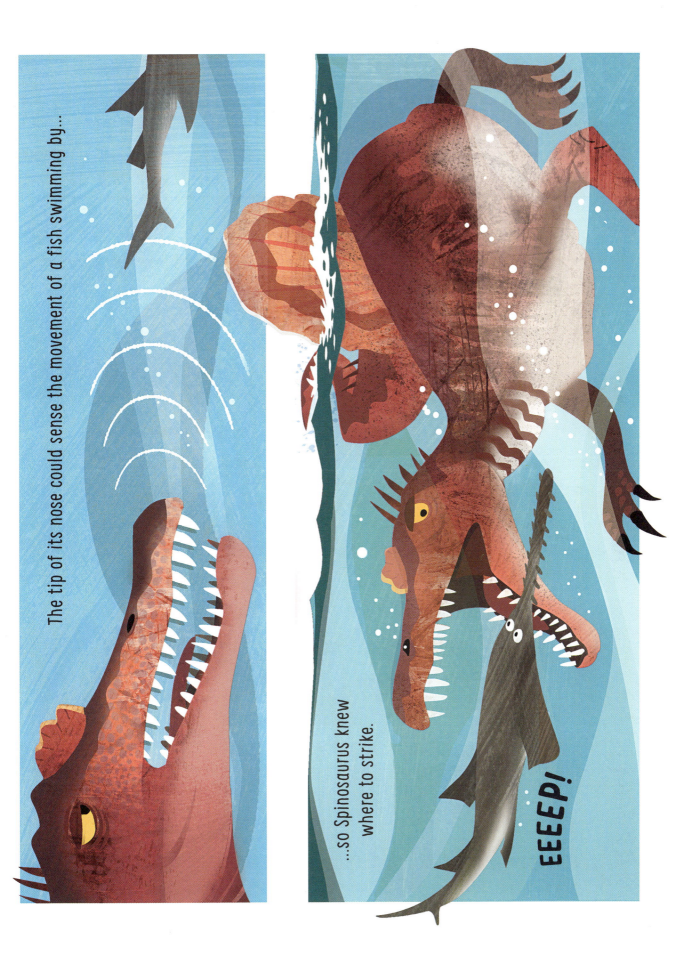

The tip of its nose could sense the movement of a fish swimming by...

...so Spinosaurus knew where to strike.

EEEEP!

What did dinosaurs get up to in the dark?

Take a look through these night vision binoculars to see who was wide **awake**...

My turn!

EDMONTOSAURUSES

These dinosaurs didn't know night from day. Their home near the top of the planet stayed dark all winter.

Other Edmontosauruses lived where it was very warm and sunny. Scientists think that they waited for darkness to search for food, so they didn't get too hot.

The little hunter that heard its way to its next meal

Hidden inside this next dinosaur's head was a pair of amazingly sensitive **ears**.

SHUVUUIA

Its sharp hearing helped **Shuvuuia** to pinpoint insects scuttling beneath the desert sand.

Even in the pitch black of night, Shuvuuia knew exactly where to dig to find bugs to eat.

Why the first dinosaur experts had dinner inside an Iguanodon

Just 200 years ago, no one knew a single thing about dinosaurs.

People digging up dinosaur bones before then mistook them for the remains of...

...dragons

...enormous fish

...and **even** giants.

BUT IN 1842...

...British scientist Richard Owen made a huge discovery.

He worked out that three separate sets of fossils all came from the **same** group of animals. So he decided to call them **dinosaurs**.

I made up the name DINOSAUR. It means MIGHTY LIZARD in Ancient Greek.

TEN YEARS LATER...

...four life-size models of these dinosaurs went on display in London's Crystal Palace Park.

They didn't look exactly right, but they were the first ones ever seen.

These spikes actually belonged on the front feet.

TWO IGUANODONS

MEGALOSAURUS

HYLAEOSAURUS

A real Megalosaurus walked on two legs.

And the mould used to make one of the Iguanodons was the venue for a very special dinner...

...with Richard Owen and other dinosaur scientists as guests.

More soup?

Pigeon pie coming through...

The dinosaur models are still in Crystal Palace Park today.

233

Claws three times longer than bananas

Can you think what it would be like if your fingernails were to grow as long as a banana? And how about as long as three big bananas? Only then would you be a match for **Therizinosaurus**.

It had the LONGEST CLAWS of any animal ever.

Look at the size of them!

Therizinosaurus ate plants. It used its claws to hook dangling branches and pull them towards its mouth.

How Velociraptor kept its claws as sharp as needles

Velociraptor was about the size of a big dog. It had toothy jaws, a long tail, feathers all over its body and curved claws.

While hunting, Velociraptor could run quickly...

...with only two toes on each foot touching the ground.

It held its biggest claws up, so they never became blunt. They stayed perfectly pointy for pinning down little dinosaurs.

All tucked up?

Did dinosaurs sleep standing up? Did they lean against a tree? Or did they lie down? The way most dinosaurs slept is a mystery — but that's not the case for a little dinosaur called **Mei**.

Before drifting off to sleep, Mei nestled down on top of its legs.

It turned its head, and tucked it under one arm...

...and wrapped its tail around its body.

Two fossils show Mei fast asleep in this position.

While you sleep, your eyes often start to twitch.
This happens whenever you see things in your dreams.

Many animals' eyes do this in
their sleep, so it's possible that
sleeping dinosaurs' eyes twitched, too.

Maybe Mei dreamed
of hunting insects...

The creatures that lived on dinosaurs

If dinosaurs had looked very, very closely, they'd have spotted tiny insects clinging to their feathers.

The insects had short antennae on their heads and strong mouthparts. They nibbled on dinosaur feathers for food.

Eww!

Scientists know about these insects because they've found a few of them trapped inside pieces of **amber**. They're a type of fossil, too.

See the dots...
Each one is an insect!

AMBER

But what's amber and how did they get in there?

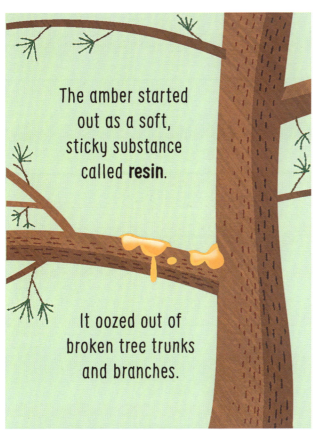

The amber started out as a soft, sticky substance called **resin**.

It oozed out of broken tree trunks and branches.

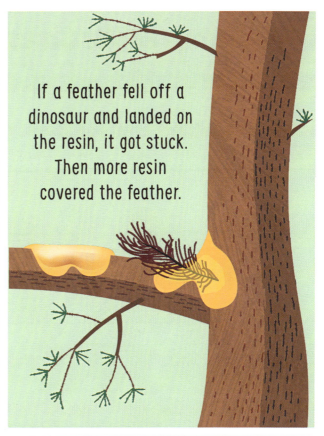

If a feather fell off a dinosaur and landed on the resin, it got stuck. Then more resin covered the feather.

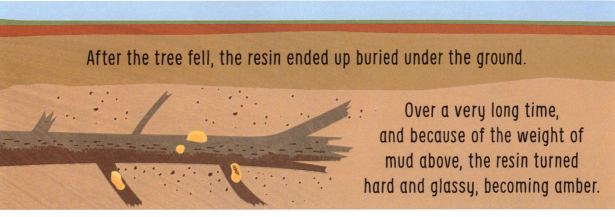

After the tree fell, the resin ended up buried under the ground.

Over a very long time, and because of the weight of mud above, the resin turned hard and glassy, becoming amber.

Lots of things from dinosaur times have been spotted in amber, such as...

ANTS

FLOWERS

CRABS

MOSQUITOS

...as well as a baby dinosaur's tail.

Bite marks, bruises and wounds... OUCH

Stand back! **Fights** between dinosaurs could turn pretty ugly...

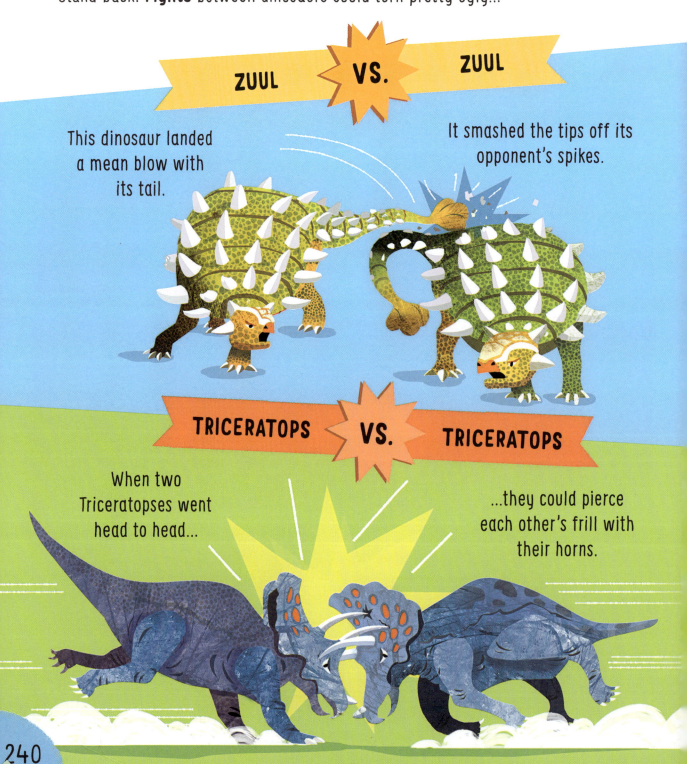

ZUUL VS. **ZUUL**

This dinosaur landed a mean blow with its tail.

It smashed the tips off its opponent's spikes.

TRICERATOPS VS. **TRICERATOPS**

When two Triceratopses went head to head...

...they could pierce each other's frill with their horns.

Dinosaur-free skies...

Every kind of dinosaur lived on land. But if they ever looked up, they'd have seen **pterosaurs**, like these ones, flying in the air.

Little pterosaurs hunted insects.

ANUROGNATHUS

Bigger pterosaurs swooped down to catch fish or squid.

RHAMPHORHYNCHUS

...and dinosaur-free seas

Phew. Nothing scary here.

Not exactly... In dinosaur times, there were sharks, as well as creatures called plesiosaurs and mosasaurs that lived underwater.

SQAULICORAX

This type of shark no longer exists.

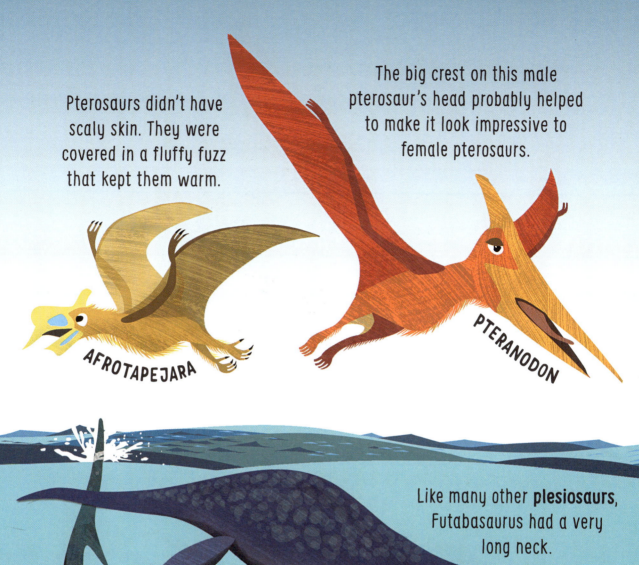

Pterosaurs didn't have scaly skin. They were covered in a fluffy fuzz that kept them warm.

The big crest on this male pterosaur's head probably helped to make it look impressive to female pterosaurs.

AFROTAPEJARA

PTERANODON

Like many other **plesiosaurs**, Futabasaurus had a very long neck.

FUTABASAURUS

TYLOSAURUS

Mosasaurs, such as Tylosaurus, had strong enough jaws to chomp on sea turtles the size of cars.

Dinosaur skull secrets

Amazing machines called CT scanners help doctors to see inside their patients' bodies. They can also reveal things about dinosaurs, such as what's inside their **skulls**...

CT SCANNER

CT SCANNER IMAGE

When the skull goes into the scanner, a computer makes lots of pictures. Together, they reconstruct the shape and size of the **brain** from the hollow space that it used to fill.

Can you help me scan this SARMIENTOSAURUS skull next, please?

ACROCANTHOSAURUS

BURIOLESTES

STEGOSAURUS

CT scans show that big dinosaurs didn't have particularly big brains.

...and **Stegosaurus's** brain was only the size of a sausage.

Sarmientosaurus's brain was smaller than an orange...

There's a rounded part of the brain that works to detect smells.

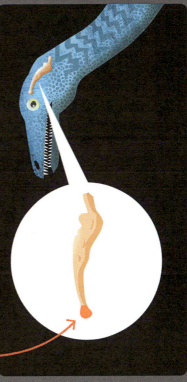

...so it probably had a much stronger sense of smell than **Buriolestes**.

This part is much bigger in **Acrocanthosaurus**...

Four heads are better than one

Life in the desert was tough for **Protoceratops** — especially when it was young.

Finding plants to eat in this dry, rocky landscape was a struggle. And there was always the looming threat of a bloodthirsty **Tarbosaurus**.

That's why young Protoceratopses joined forces in small groups.

They could search for food together and keep all their eyes peeled for danger.

Can we help? I think I saw some more leaves that way.

Underground hideaway

Oryctodromeus was hard to spot in its woodland home — unless you knew where to look...

Anyone there?

Oryctodromeus dug a **burrow** into the ground...

...where it and its babies could stay safe and warm.

Going out with a BANG

And then one day, 66 million years ago, **disaster** struck.

An **asteroid** — a giant space rock — hurtled towards Planet Earth.

It was even bigger than a mountain and landed with an almighty **CRASH**.

The dinosaurs didn't stand a chance.

The blast shook the ground around the world and churned up nightmare waves.

THESCELOSAURUS

Uh oh...

Hot dust tumbled from the sky, burying dinosaurs and sparking forest fires.

TRICERATOPS

Oh no!

There's nothing left for me to eat!

CHENANISAURUS

Then darkness fell for the next ten years. Great clouds of ash blocked out almost all the sunlight.

Was EVERYTHING wiped out?

No! Some animals hid underground or in seas and rivers. And seeds from plants survived to grow again. But that was the end of the dinosaurs.

Not quite the end...

The dinosaurs in these frames are part of a group called **theropods**. They're no longer around, of course, but every single **bird** in the world is a living theropod.

Yes, birds are the **one type of dinosaur** that's still around, flapping, pecking, hovering, squawking and chirping.

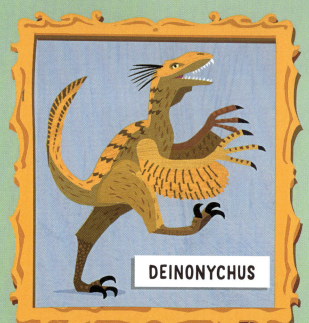

DEINONYCHUS

MACAW

CASSOWARY

They're all our LONG-LOST cousins on the wall.

KINGFISHER

FINCH

CURLEW

I bet you'll never look at birds in the same way again.

YI

ANCHIORNIS

Unlike most birds, Yi and Anchiornis couldn't fly. But they might have glided between branches in trees.

CRANE

PEREGRINE FALCON

Goodbye, Tyrannosaurus rex! Hello, Tyrannosaurus hen!

CHICKEN

EMPEROR PENGUIN

251

Glossary

algae – tiny plants that grow in water or damp places

alveoli – tiny balloon-like parts of your lungs that fill with air when you breathe

amber – a yellow-brown fossil that used to be resin

Antarctic – the icy land and sea near the South Pole

antennae – feelers on the head of an insect

appendix – a pouch inside your tummy the size of your little finger

Arctic – the icy land and sea near the North Pole

asteroid – a lump of rock in space

astronaut – a person who travels into space

astronomer – a person who studies space, especially stars

bacteria – tiny living things, some are good and some are germs

billion – a thousand million

black hole – a hole in space with gravity so strong nothing can escape its pull

blowhole – a breathing hole on top of a whale's head

blubber – a thick layer of fat under the skin of seals and whales

brain – a squishy organ in your head that controls almost everything you do

bristle – a stiff, threadlike spike

burrow – a hole or tunnel under the ground where some animals live

comet – a ball of frozen gas and rock that travels around the solar system

coprolite – a fossilized dinosaur poo

corals – sea creatures that form rock-like structures

crest – a fleshy mound or feathery tuft on an animal's head

Cretaceous – the time when the last dinosaurs lived

disability – a condition of the body or mind that makes it more difficult for someone to do certain things

DNA – a set of instructions, found everywhere in your body, that decides how your body looks and how it works

fangs – sharp, pointed teeth

fins – flat parts of a fish, whale or dolphin's body that stick out

fossil – a rock-like thing left behind by ancient animals or plants

fossilized – turned into a fossil

frill – a bony or fleshy flap behind an animal's head

galaxy – a huge group of billions of stars. Our galaxy is the Milky Way.

gas – a thing like air that isn't solid like rock or liquid like water

gas giant – a huge planet made of gases

germs – tiny things – some alive, some not – that can make you ill

gills – body parts that fish and some animals have for breathing underwater

gravity – a force that pulls things toward it. The bigger the object, the stronger its gravity

heart – an organ made from muscle that pumps blood around your body

heart attack – when someone's heart stops working properly

hormones – chemicals released by your body that tell it what to do

horn – a hard, pointed spike that grows from an animal's head

ice giant – a huge planet made of heavy gases known as ices

Jurassic – the time between the Triassic and the Cretaceous

kidneys – two organs in your lower back that clean your blood and make wee

light year – the distance light travels in a year, used for measuring space outside the solar system

liver – an organ that does lots of important jobs, such as storing energy and releasing hormones

lungs – two organs in your chest that breathe for you

meteor shower – fireworks in the sky, usually from a comet

migration – a journey made by animals in search of food, better weather and places to have babies

moon – an object that orbits a planet, a **moonlet** is a very small one

mosasaur – an ancient sea creature with a wide tail

moss – a soft plant that grows on rocks and tree bark

mucus – slimy snotty watery stuff inside your nose and other organs

muscle – a body part used for moving

nerves – thread-like things that carry messages from your body to your brain and from your brain to your body

operation – when doctors cut open the body to make repairs inside

orbit – to go around something. Planets go around stars and their path is called an orbit, too

organ – a part of your body that does a particular set of jobs

ossicones – bony bumps on a giraffe's head

oviraptorosaur – a type of dinosaur that had feathers

oxygen – a gas in the air that you need to breathe to stay alive

planet – a large, round object that orbits the Sun – for example Earth. Planets orbiting other stars are called exoplanets.

plate – a thick, bony part on a dinosaur's body

plesiosaur – an ancient sea creature with a long or short neck

pterosaur – an ancient animal that could fly

red blood cells – tiny round red blobs in your blood that deliver oxygen around your body

rover – a kind of robot used to explore the surface of a moon or planet

sauropod – a type of big dinosaur

scales – little parts over an animal's skin that protect its body

school – a group of fish swimming in the same direction

silk – a fine, sticky thread made by spiders and some baby insects

solar system, the – the Sun and all the planets – and everything else – that orbit it

solar wind – energy from the Sun that 'blows' like wind. **Stellar wind** is the same energy from other stars

space station – a spaceship in orbit where astronauts can live and work

sponge – a living thing with lots of holes that grows on the sea floor

star – an enormous ball of burning gases that gives off light and heat

star nursery – a part of space where new stars form

star system – a star and everything that orbits it

stomach – an organ in your tummy that holds food after you swallow it

supernova – the huge explosion when a big star dies

surgery – see **operation**

swarm – a group of flying animals

telescope – a device for seeing faraway things, such as stars, in detail

theropod – a type of dinosaur with hollow bones

tonsils – two small organs at the back of your mouth

track – a mark left behind by an animal when it moves

trench – a deep crack in the ground or sea floor

Triassic – the time when the first dinosaurs lived

universe, the – everything in space

venom – a type of poison that some animals use to kill, stun or blind other animals

vertebrae – small bones that join together to make up the backbone

womb – the organ where babies grow before they are born

Index

Expert advisers:
Your Body: Doctor Salma Ahmed
Space: UK Space Agency and astronomer Nick Howes
Animals: Professor David Macdonald
Dinosaurs: Dr. Andre Rowe

Editor: Ruth Brocklehurst
Managing designers: Helen Lee and Stephen Moncrieff